Native American
Stories of the Sacred

T0165854

Other books in the
SkyLight Illuminations Series

Native American Stories of the Sacred

Annotated & Explained

Retold and Annotated by Evan T. Pritchard

Walking Together, Finding the Way ®
SKYLIGHT PATHS®
PUBLISHING

Native American Stories of the Sacred:
Annotated & Explained

2015 Quality Paperback Edition

Library of Congress Cataloging-in-Publication Data
Pritchard, Evan T., 1955–
Native American stories of the sacred : annotated & explained : retold, annotated & explained / by Evan T. Pritchard.
   p. cm. — (SkyLight illuminations)
Includes bibliographical references. (p.   ).
ISBN-13: 978-1-59473-112-9 (pbk.)
ISBN-10: 1-59473-112-8 (pbk.)
1. Indians of North America—Folklore. 2. Indian mythology—North America. I. Title. II. Series.
E98.F6P75 2005
398'.41'08997—dc22   2005016943
ISBN 978-1-59473-366-6 (eBook)

Manufactured in the United States of America

Cover design: Walter C. Bumford III
Cover art: Jason Stitt
Interior art: Joanne Plamondon

SkyLight Paths Publishing is creating a place where people of different spiritual traditions come together for challenge and inspiration, a place where we can help each other understand the mystery that lies at the heart of our existence.

SkyLight Paths sees both believers and seekers as a community that increasingly transcends traditional boundaries of religion and denomination—people wanting to learn from each other, *walking together, finding the way.*

SkyLight Paths, "Walking Together, Finding the Way," and colophon are trademarks of LongHill Partners, Inc., registered in the U.S. Patent and Trademark Office.

Walking Together, Finding the Way
Published by SkyLight Paths Publishing
A Division of LongHill Partners, Inc.
An Imprint of Turner Publishing Company
4507 Charlotte Avenue, Suite 100
Nashville, TN 37209
Tel: (615) 255-2665
www.skylightpaths.com

Contents □

Preface ☐

I would like to begin this book of sacred journeys with the first words of "The Mud Diver Story": "*Gutakameo laawatay,*" which is Munsee for "One day, a long time ago … " It is a great way to begin a story and, perhaps, an entire world. This book contains a number of Native American stories—those that have spiritual significance to me and, to some extent, to the world at large. They are meant to be enjoyed and shared. Stories cross over cultural borders quicker than carrier pigeons, and this is as true now as it has been for centuries. This fact helps unite all of us, even as we retain our individual traditions and beliefs.

These are not "sacred stories" per se, intended only for the sweat lodge, high ceremony, or for retelling only within certain lodges. Many of *those* stories go on for four days and would not make sense to most readers even with annotations. These "stories *of* the sacred," if we can call them that, are wisdom tales for children and adults that contain elegantly simple illustrations of time-tested teachings that refer to that which is sacred. Most of these insights are so universal and eternal that they have been noticed and preserved in stories worldwide. However, each story contains cultural references that need to be explained for the full meaning to emerge, and each has an unmistakable Native American flavor, which needs no explanation at all.

Although I am a person of Native American and Celtic ancestry, and consider myself to have been raised more or less in the values and beliefs of the Mi'kmaq traditions, I have always been keenly interested in how people around the world perceive God and themselves spiritually. This book, perhaps more than my previous publications on Native American culture, reflects that interest, which has been an unwavering passion for me since early childhood.

I learned from an early age that all human beings are our relations, as are the animals, plants, fish, moon, and stars. I also understood that any of these—a bird, a child, an old man—could become a messenger to us at a certain moment, and so I listened to people of all denominations and kept praying for good messages and for good visions. It is not surprising, then, that I soon came into contact with organized religion.

Although I grew up within walking distance of my spiritual temple— the woods and hills of Maryland—I was also not far from a world cultural center, Washington, D.C., which in the 1960s was filled with a wide variety of spiritual activities. Religious leaders of all stripes and colors came to visit Washington and speak out on "what was wrong with America." Before I drove a car—the modern-day coming of age initiation for urban Indians—I'd already had the opportunity to meet and ask questions of Martin Buber, the Talmudic philosopher; the Reverend David Eaton, a black minister, talk show host, and friend of Martin Luther King Jr.; Isaac Bashevis Singer, the Jewish storyteller; Sri Chin Moy, the Pakistani poet and yogi; Brahmachari Keith, a disciple of Paramahansa Yogananda; and Dr. Mael Melvin, an astrophysicist at Temple University and one of the founders of the Transcendental Meditation movement. I also learned a lot from the monks at Catholic University, where I studied religion and philosophy as part of the regular curriculum, and from street people who had earned divine insight from hard suffering on the front lines of life.

It was a wonderful way to spend one's youth, and I learned that many of the negative stereotypes we hear about people whose religions are "different" are not true, at least not for those who have been truly touched by the God of their ancestors, be it Allah, Brahma, or Jehovah. I found my teachers everywhere, in all traditions, and learned to call them my friends. It didn't hurt that my father read to us from Joseph Campbell's expansive multicultural book *Hero with a Thousand Faces* at the dinner table when we were in high school.

But outside of my own family, none of my teachers was Native American. For much of that time, Native American elders had been excluded from this multicultural dialogue about God. And yet, all along, the Native American teaching "We all belong here; we are all part of the great hoop of life" had helped form the foundation of religious tolerance in America and Canada. It is part of certain Native American teachings that different races and cultures are like the colors of the rainbow: they blend and yet retain their distinct identity. This Native principle for an inclusive, healthy society was enjoyed to a certain extent by most North Americans, yet not by the Native North Americans themselves. In my youth, I applied that rainbow principle to religion and was richly rewarded. I feel it is appropriate for religion to offer that colorful invitation to Native Americans to foster a dialogue that is well overdue.

Edward S. Curtis, the photographer and creator of the twenty-volume illustrated collection *The North American Indian* published between 1907 and 1930, wrote, in that curious backward-looking style of his time that presumed the demise of Native American culture:

> What might we, Americans, have made of the Indians? : "The Indians could have given us physical vigor which must be one of the foundations of any lasting and important strength; they could have helped us in the creation of literature, for they were marvelous in the beauty of their free, poetic thoughts full of imagery such as white men have never known. Their souls were those of poets. They could have helped us in our music, for theirs was a real part of their lives, a genuine expression of emotion. They could have aided us vastly in our decorative art. And in a broad sense, they could have helped us in our morals, for in all their dealing they were fair until we taught them theft and lying."[1]

In fact, when we put aside romantic notions that Native American culture cannot survive modernity, we can hear more clearly the voices of contemporary Native Americans, including visionaries like vice-presidential candidate Winona LaDuke and Colorado senator Ben Nighthorse Campbell, who are explaining—and demonstrating—how many of these teachings have as much relevance and impact today as they ever had.

In my brazen youth I was somewhat outspoken on the subject of God, and, looking back, I realize that most of my ideas were derived from my Native American heritage, though I would never have said so. Inspired teachers from many faiths treated my insights with respect and openness, and, just as I was invited into the rainbow by others, I learned to trust the interfaith process of dialogue and invite others into my "Native American" rainbow as well. When the Sixteenth Karmapa, head of the Kagyu lineage of Tibetan Buddhism, came to Washington, I dreamed that I met him and all his attending lamas, even though I didn't know who he was at the time of my dream. I read about him in the newspaper the next day and followed up on it years later. I ended up "taking refuge" (a non-exclusive kind of confirmation) with one of those lamas whose picture was in the paper. My study of Tibetan Buddhism led me to the Himalayas and back, and then face-to-face with the Dalai Lama, whose teachings about tolerance and forgiveness while courageously speaking the truth have inspired me both to forgive in my heart the removal of Native people from their homelands and the deliberate suppression of their culture and, at the same time, to openly speak the truth as I know it.

Then I learned to drive! Soon after I had learned this sacred thing, I got a car, and Spirit used that vehicle to lead me to New York City where I had the precious opportunity to serve, question, and learn from excellent and well-known spiritual teachers and mystics in service to the Great Mystery. Although I am best known today as a spokesperson for Native American culture, these people inspired me in my vocation as an interfaith minister and professor of world religions. All my experiences in New York were an education in the intangible value of human life, the preciousness of every breath we breathe, and the joy and exuberance that comes with real inspiration.

In 1989, when I finally connected with the Native American elders I had been looking for all those years, I was able to immediately see for myself how truly gifted they were and how valuable they could be to the world community. The wisdom I had hunted for all that time had been in my backyard all along. Meeting and talking with outstanding teachers of all nations had helped me recognize that here was the very thing that had been missing from my own life and, to a troubling extent, from the worldwide interfaith dialogue as well. I saw that many of the languages and oral traditions were dying out and began to write down what I could in order to preserve that indigenous knowledge. I am now extending that to story as well. Constance DeJong once said, "Legends that are passed down by word of mouth are legends lost." In our society, that seems to be more and more the situation, although it was not always so.

One unifying feature of Native American belief is the concept of the "Red Road," though each tribe and nation also has its own name for it. Black Elk speaks of the Red Road in the book *The Sacred Pipe*. In Mi'kmaq, the "way of truth" is called *agulamz*. In Cherokee, the "way of good" is *dohi* (*do-hi*). The Hopi speak of the good red road that leads to a world that is healthy and safe for raising children. The Navajo call it "the beauty way," which I have learned to live more effectively by returning to my own traditions.

I have found no one word in English that truly describes this "way." However, a similar version of this word exists in at least a dozen ancient cultures all over the world. If you research these enigmatic words for many years, as I have done, I think you will come to the same conclusion. Each eludes an exact definition, yet each invokes, substantially, "the right way."

In China, the word *Tao* means "the path." Although they say "The Tao that can be spoken of is not the Tao," this word implies more than simply wise ways to behave in human interactions—it also encompasses "the path" of things in nature and in the realm of the eternal. This is remarkably close to the fullness of meanings implied by the Red Road. Indeed, some Native American elders who have never read a book have spoken words about the Red Road that almost perfectly match those of Lao Tzu, the Chinese sage to whom we credit the *Tao te Ching*.

Another example from Hindu religion, more correctly called Sanatana Dharma, is the word *dharma* (*dhamma* in the Pali Canon), which originally carried all the same associations as Tao and the Red Road. Later, possibly around the time of Ashoka, dharma took on the additional meaning of *law* as a way of demanding that people actually put these principles into practice.

In Greek, the word *dikaion* has these same meanings but is associated with the balance of action in the universe that Plato defined as "universal justice." This is not the justice of human laws, but a principle in the cosmos that predates humankind, like gravity. This word appeared in the Septuagint, then in the Greek New Testament, was eventually translated into Latin as *justitia* and, in time, into English not as *justness*—which would have been logical—but as *righteousness,* which might be associated with self-righteousness and judgmentalism, rather than with the "straight and narrow way" or the right way to live. However, it does refer to "being on the right path" when taken literally, which leads us back again to the Red Road, "the right way."

In the Celtic language family there is a word that is sometimes spelled *Fi-rhinne* (pronounced with a rolled *r*), which is associated with virtue, but which can be interpreted in a variety of ways: One with Fi-rhinne would be courageous, forthright, reliable, and truthful.

In Islam, the word *Shari'a* means "the path," but, like dharma, came to also mean "law," and is the basis of Islamic law. In Egypt the word *ma'at* referred to universal justice, but also to virtue, similar to the Celtic word. During the rise of Pharaoic power, the Pharaohs took exclusive control of ma'at and said that only they could understand all the levels of meaning of ma'at, or could truly be virtuous. At some point, the universal principle called ma'at became embodied by the goddess *Ma'at,* who was the forerunner of the Greek goddess of justice, whose picture is displayed prominently in many courtrooms in America. When Egyptians went to the world of the dead, they had to face Ma'at. His or her heart was removed and placed in her balanced scales, where it was weighed against a falcon's feather; if it was heavier than the feather, the person had to face Ma'at's judgment. This recalls the Native American saying, "Enjoy life but leave no tracks." We need to take things lightheartedly in order to pass beyond the gates of Ma'at's temple. A lighthearted person does not leave a trail of injustices behind.

I have been told that the Hebrew word *Halakhah* was in ancient times the word that referred to the good way. Not enough people were able to grasp for themselves what the good way really was or how a good person should act, so the various commandments in the Torah—the first five books of the Hebrew Bible—were made into a list of 613 *mitzvot* (plural for mitzvah, "commandment"). This list can be found in the Talmud, although there is more than one version.

In Sami, the language of the Sami people (who are often incorrectly called "Lapps" and whose territory is often incorrectly called Lapland), the pathfinder, or wayshower, is called the *noiadi*. In Slavic (Russian) the word *doroga* means "roadway," and is related to *drog,* the Old Chinese for Tao, and related to the English word "duty."[2] However the Russian word *put'* (pronounced "poodt") today carries the mystical meaning of "the path we walk."

There are many more examples from all over the world of such words that have survived even though their parent languages are nearly extinct: words showing us that at one time everyone may have shared a common mystical belief in a "right way" for humankind to follow. In the film *Good Enough for Two,* Mi'kmaq canoe builder Todd Labrador relates how his father told him that in the forest, all trees may seem to be separate, but underneath the ground, they are holding hands—their roots intertwine in a great web of life, regardless of species. In a similar way, I feel that the Red Road teachings and the Native American spiritual philosophy as a whole offer the people of the world a view of these common "Taoistic" roots and a source of inspiration for re-examining their own natural origins, which are intertwined.

Following the Red Road, I founded the Center for Algonquin Culture, a nonprofit organization in service to the elders of the Algonquin (and other) nations, to help them bring their spiritual message more effectively to the mass media. Some elders do not wish for notoriety, feeling that it would interfere with their work. Others, such as William Commanda, who holds the Seven Fires Wampum Belt that embodies prophecies given to the Algonquin people over 700 years ago (and who has met with the Dalai Lama on several occasions), and Eddie Benton Benaise, the Medicine Chief of the Three Fires Midewiwin Lodge (and who has a master's degree in comparative religion), are becoming well known to the public. There are many others. The change is about to happen.

William Commanda recently wrote:

> My peoples have been crushed for a long time.... We see churches, cathedrals, synagogues, temples and mosques reflecting the great diversity of cultures here [in North America] but there is still no place where indigenous peoples can gather together in the spirit of unity that used to mark our heritage.
>
> Over recent years, I have ... said that Turtle Island would not find true peace until the relationship with the first peoples of this land was healed and we occupied our rightful position in the heart of this country.... But my ancestors used to say the most nutritious walnuts emerge after the coldest winter. In my mind, it is the indigenous peoples who hold the seeds for a vision of inclusion and collective sharing, respect, and responsibility.
>
> [This is why,] with the commencement of the United Nations Decade for a Culture of Peace, I began to pursue the work of developing a vision for a fully inclusive indigenous peace-building cultural centre on Victoria Island [near Parliament in Ottawa, Ontario, Canada].

The essential message that unifies Native American wisdom teaching is clear: "The earth does not belong to us; we belong to the earth." Whether or not Chief Seattle really said this is disputed, but it makes no difference; thousands of Native Americans had said it before he was ever born, and thousands have said it since, and I'm saying it now. It is a teaching that is not totally unknown within the great world religions. The Arabic word *hilafa*, for example, refers to a stewardship "bestowed in trust" in Islam; and in the Qur'an (10:14), the angels state, "Thus we have made you to succeed one another as stewards on the earth, that

We might behold how you acquit yourselves."[3] *Shomrei Adamah* means "Guardians of the Earth" in Hebrew and refers to a group within Judaism that places emphasis on the Jewish traditions that honor the earth, such as *Tu B'shevat*, the Jewish New Year of the Trees, and *Bal Tashchit*, the biblical prohibition against wasteful behavior. Each major faith has one or more branches or leaders who do honor the earth in this way, but typically these groups and leaders are misunderstood—and marginalized—by their own religious organizations.

In this book, I see a narrow path along which to bring others to a place where they can see that Chief Seattle's message is an essentially *religious* message. By pointing out concerns and sensibilities that Native American stories share with the sacred texts and stories of religions across the globe, I will show that respect and love for the earth is the strong, unmistakable message that Native American spirituality brings to the world table—a message that has never been more needed than now.

The path of honoring the earth is not an easy one. Although it promises seven generations of gain, it does require short-term sacrifices. It has never been a popular path, and not enough people have walked it. In order to truly change our destructive ways, we need to have an emotional connection to Mother Earth, perhaps even a religious zeal about our relationship with her. Almost all of the elders I have worked with have this zeal. Sometimes it surprises me still. This emotional connection affects every aspect of traditional culture, and unless people of all cultures and races learn to embrace this ancient teaching as their own indigenous ancestors once did, I fear that we are not to last as a species. We need to pay attention to the hell on earth we could be creating out of the paradise that is God's handiwork.

I hope these stories provide an entertaining and inviting way for readers to form a deeper understanding of Native American spirituality and Native American culture, and of how the wisdom of the words "The earth does not belong to us; we belong to the earth" are uniquely inherent to both.

Introduction □

In the Native American Medicine Wheel teachings, there are four cardinal directions on the surface of our Mother Earth, representing "the fourness of things." According to this teaching, everything can be seen as having four sides, four dimensions, four categories. This teaching is often illustrated by a visual aid, such as a willow hoop with crossed sticks inside or a circle of stones on the ground with a cross of stones in the middle corresponding to east, south, west, and north. Essentially, these four sections of the Wheel represent the four parts of the self: the soul or spirit, the mind and speech, the heart and self-expression, and the body and its purification. There is a male and female aspect to each.

A religion—whatever its origin—is more than a spiritual path: it also invariably contains a philosophy, numerous folk customs, and a wealth of stories or teaching tales. The spirituality of a given religion, including meditation practices and revealed teachings, arises out of the depths of the illumined soul; the philosophy behind the spiritual message arises from the clarity of mind that a true religious experience produces; the traditions, folk customs, health practices, and artifacts that affect the physical body arise from the religious culture; and the wealth of stories, teaching tales, myths, and legends—not to mention the poetry and songs—that each religion preserves come from the heart of the faithful. Each Native American subculture has all these, so Native American spirituality in each of its forms could be compared with every world religion point for point.

In fact, comparing Native American spiritual philosophy, spiritual customs, and—most relevant to this book—spiritual stories with those of other cultures across the globe could give us an objective basis for meaningful cross-cultural comparisons without stereotyping, generalizing, perpetuating misconceptions, and without resorting to calling spiritual beliefs and practices "religion," a word that most Native Americans agree does not fit their personal experience with the Great Medicine (or the Great Mystery), which is without scripture or edifice. Native American spirituality, which was first discovered—and apparently taken seriously—by the Vikings one thousand years ago, needs to be taken seriously again. We can get to know the Native American spiritual landscape "bird by bird," to quote an expression from writer Anne Lamott—or in this case, story by story. Doing this will deepen our understanding of ourselves, regardless of our culture of origin.

For now I am grateful to be able to create a context in which the not-always-obvious sacredness of a handful of Native American stories can reveal itself, one story at a time, to readers from all backgrounds and cultures. This book offers an opportunity to close a culture gap, to create a context in which Native American stories of the sacred can be not only understood by outsiders, but compared with stories from the world's religions, specifically from the Jewish and Christian traditions (which have touched all our lives in some way), without forgetting the Taoist, Buddhist, Celtic, Hindu, and Islamic stories and teachings.

It has always struck me as odd that so many Americans know much more about the beliefs of Taoists in Taiwan and Taipei, Buddhists in Sri Lanka, and Hindus in Srinigar than they do about comparable Native American beliefs and enlightenment traditions that were brought to fruition literally in their own backyards. When I speak of how important it is for Algonquin and Siouian pipe carriers to grow their hair long, some people will be puzzled; they will ask, "What does growing your hair have to do with God?" But if I compare it to the beliefs of the Nazirites in the Bible, of whom it is said, "The crown of his God is upon his head" (Samson was a Nazirite), they might say, "Oh, sure, that makes sense!"

There are countless similarities between the early ceremonial practices mentioned in the Hebrew scriptures and those of Native Americans. It doesn't mean that any Native American tribe is "the lost tribe of Israel."

Native American nations generally predate even the ancient Hebrew tribal nations of pre-Mosaic times and, according to recent discoveries, the pre-Clovis ancestors of the Algonquins date back at least to 16,000 B.C.E., if not earlier. We can't always explain why such similarities exist, except that we all are related, as the saying goes. While ceremonies may differ from place to place, the truths embraced in Native American traditions are powerful, sacred, universal, and eternal. So it stands to reason they would have parallels in all times and all places around the world.

The gap that exists today between ourselves and the essence of Native American spiritual traditions is probably larger than we tend to think, but it is the same gap that stands between ourselves and nature, between ourselves and our true spiritual self, and between ourselves and God. The gap exists not between one ancient sacred path and another, but between ourselves and the sacred, between our media-saturated lives and the lives of our own ancestors, between our artificial lives and the mysterious forces of nature. If we really understood the heart of Judaism as Moses did, the heart of Christianity as Jesus did, the heart of Islam as Muhammad did, the heart of Jainism as Mahavira did, and the heart of Buddhism as Buddha did, our understanding of Native American traditions would deepen to a comparable degree. These great teachers were close to the earth and to their own indigenous roots, as were the Lakota man Black Elk, the enlightened Lenape Delaware men Neoline and Oneeum, Chief Seattle, Chief Joseph of the Nez Perce, Sweet Medicine of the Cheyenne, the Peacemaker who came to the Iroquois/Haudenosaunee, and Wovoka of the Paiute, to name a few. If we sat under a Bodhi tree for a while and waited for enlightenment, we would, at the very least, feel a lot closer to the rhythms of nature, and that alone would help us understand these "strange" Native American spiritual tales.

So, if Native American spirituality has so much in common with other traditions, why can't we just add "Native American" to the list of world religions and proclaim them equal? Because it is not a unified religion. Native Americans have no dogma, other than "thou shalt have no dogma," and no central unifying creed, other than "take care of Mother Earth, and Father Sky, and they will take care of you." There are numerous other common beliefs that we can presume most traditional native people lean toward: the sacredness of the circle; the belief in a spirit world; the importance of ritual and of making offerings; and the importance of purification, of prayer, of healing, of honesty, of community, of seeking visions, and of communication with animals. However, Native American communities developed in different places and at different times and have diverged greatly since the fifteenth century, influenced by different European encroachments. Today the differences between tribes and nations are as significant as the similarities. Tribes and nations have become proud of their own individual and local insights and won't easily give them up to jump into someone else's game bag in the name of religion. It is said, "God is too big for one religion," and the Great Spirit is too big for one Native American view to dominate.

The Jewish and Christian traditions have always been celebrated for presenting a single, unified, and definitive picture of the cosmos, most aspects of which can be clearly visualized, verbalized, and written down. But the decentralized yet all-inclusive tradition of the Native Americans, most of which cannot be written down, has always defied definitions and final answers. It has no one center and therefore is organic, not cosmic, at least not in the conventional sense. It is oriented toward seeing the way things are rather than the way we think they should be, and it does not assume the universe is designed in a way that the mind can understand—hence the term *Great Mystery*. Not surprisingly, there are certain traditions within Christianity that echo the Native American. The *docta ignorantia* of Catholic theology states that God can only be known by what God is not, a teaching completely in agreement with the Vedic view of Brahma and with the Native American view of the Great Mystery.[1]

Native traditions are no less God-filled for insisting on these maddening absences of linear theological structure, and they are no less simple to live by just because they allow for such complexity in the real world.

The Native American ancestors seem to have understood the craving of the human mind to explain everything and to tie it all up in one neat package, right or wrong, and long ago decided to sabotage that possibility at every turn so that no one could create a religion out of it. Instead, what was created was a way of life that nurtures deeply religious experiences, which is a different thing.

The simplest explanation I have ever heard of Native American theology is this: We human beings stand halfway between heaven and earth. Father Sky (or Sun) is distant but wise, and keeps the stars and planets on their rightful paths. Mother Earth is always under our feet, always trying to keep us from getting sick with all her helpful medicines and herbs, always loving us. And we are the baby—when we stand in sacred space and when we are in ceremony. We have a right to be here. We are part of all that is holy, part of a holy trinity. That's it. If you are looking for a central point from which to begin your exploration of Native American spirituality, start here, but then abandon it as soon as you outgrow it.

Teaching tales are often like parables, but, unlike the parables in the Christian Bible that comprise a large percentage of Jesus's teachings, the Native American stories are usually left unexplained. This is done out of respect for both the intelligence of the listener and the Great Mystery. However, stories are also as three-dimensional as the objects and creatures that inhabit them, and so no matter how much you explain them, there is always a great deal left over to wonder at and ponder over, becoming clear to us later, when we are ready, each according to his or her own capacity. Everyone gets what they can from them, and the rest is left to dawn on you later.

For this reason I will not try to be comprehensive or overly academic in my annotation. I will leave some mysteries unsolved, and some comparisons unmade, remembering that my little piece of the puzzle, which I have struggled to acquire, is like a teaspoonful of water to the thirsty, and that we are already fish swimming in the sea. As Kabir once said, "I laugh when I hear the fish are thirsty!"

Creation Stories

"In the beginning ... " is the way we might expect the first story to unfold. However, in Native American Dream Time—which is when most stories and legends happen—there is no beginning, and there is no end. Everything is cyclical. In a great number of Native American tongues there is no word for "hello"; we just say, "How has the world been treating you?" There is no word for "good-bye"; we just say, "See you again." The sacred hoop of life is unending, and anyone looking for *the* Creation story will be disappointed. In fact, the word *the* doesn't exist in a vast majority of Native American languages, so the best we can do is to find perhaps *a* Creation story that has meaning to us.

There is no one beginning moment of Creation, like the seven days mentioned in Genesis. In fact, in Native American terms, Creation is happening now, and we are a part of it. Today is that day. In many Native tongues, a word for *day* is "a sun," but that is also a word for a long era of many years. Native American "history" goes back to well before the beginning of "time," and some Native people adamantly refuse to acknowledge this thing called "time," or at least the conventional notions about it. Native history goes back to before the beginning of writing, for what is writing to a hunting and gathering people? It goes back to before the discovery of fire, as Native stories remember when there was no fire. In fact, it goes back to the beginning of language, for this is when the first story was told. And in that first story, the storyteller probably began with the words, "A long, long time ago ... "

There is no date of Creation and no single event that has equal significance for all. The tales and beliefs of Native Americans are part of a spiritual way of life, some of which may be considered "religious." However, that religion is different for each cultural group, for each nation, and even for each person. There is generally no dogma that unifies the people. Instead, they are unified by their love and interrelationships, their language, history, and mutual needs, even if they disagree about beliefs. For example, it is possible for a Shawnee man or woman to practice—with great zeal—the Shawnee spiritual traditions in a way that no one else on earth is currently practicing or has practiced for a hundred years, and yet if that way is a good way and does not violate the core tradition, that person will be respected.

There are many versions of each of these Creation stories and, in an oral tradition, that is as it should be. However, to commit them to writing I had to choose one or, in some cases, link together two or three. The emphasis here is on the spirit of the story and the teachings that one might derive from it. If I have changed a word here and there, it is because I put my heart into it.

When Christian missionaries first came to the Native Americans with their miraculous stories from biblical scripture, there was some confusion and embarrassment among the people as to whether these teaching tales were to be taken as fiction or nonfiction. Intertribal storytelling, which was always quite widespread, had already taught them the importance of being diplomatic about such things. When told that the Bible stories were true, many Natives, raised on similar stories, accepted them as teaching tales to be taken as true. In fact, the incredible tales of the trickster Wehix-amukes among the Lenape are considered to be nonfiction among the true believers, and fiction among those who have their doubts. Therefore, some will speak of Wehixamukes only during the winter, and others year-round.[2] Storytellers will often guide the listener as to the proper response. If he or she says, "And that's the way it happened," you know it is presented as true. If they say "That's what the old men/women told me," you may take it as a story.

Creation is especially sacred because life is sacred. Native Americans honor that Creation, especially that aspect of Creation that European culture calls "nature," which is beyond human ability to create, and therefore was made by a higher power. Each Creation story is not just about a distant God of unimaginable power creating this and that according to some divine plan. These Creation stories are really about *you*, about your place in the universal Creation process. We don't have to look hard to find that strand of teaching that leads back into our own heart and asks us, "Why are *you* here? Who are your people? What is your personal mission in this lifetime? What is your true name? What is your language? How are you going to find that inner peace of heart that you were born with?" These last four are the four gifts from the Creator that the Ojibway speak of, and they are questions that each person can ask, regardless of background.

In many cultures, including the Native American, seven is "the number of Creation" and signifies completeness, because there are seven directions: east, south, west, north, up, down, and to the center. It is also the greatest number of generations of your own family that you are likely to meet in your lifetime; great-grandmother, grandmother, mother, sister, daughter, granddaughter, and great-granddaughter. In many tales around the world, there are seven generations from the First Man/First Woman to the first person of the next stage of Creation. As in Genesis, the significance of seven generations in Native American teachings can be either negative or positive; we must strive to think ahead as to what will benefit our offspring to the seventh generation, for if we do not, our offspring will suffer for it "intergenerationally," as modern psychologists put it.

One example of the importance of seven is the biblical story of Noah. He was the seventh-generation descendant in "the wicked bloodline of Cain," but he was also from the "good bloodline of Seth," as the two lines had started to intermarry. His father, Lamech (seventh from Adam in the line of Cain), was prideful, a self-made man, "master of his own destiny," whereas those in the line of Seth were obedient to God's will. Noah was seventh from both Cain and Seth, and so bore both the burden of Cain's sins and the benefit of Seth's wisdom. It is unfortunate that in common parlance, people mostly remember the curse of Cain and not the blessings of Seth, which were equal in the importance they played in the biblical narrative.

In Japan's Shinto Creation mythology, there are seven generations between the unnamed deities born at the time of heaven and earth's

Creation and the birth of Izanagi (male) and Izanami (female) who "solidified the earth." Amaterasu is one of their children, from whom the emperors of Japan descend.

In the much-beloved "The Mud Diver Story," we identify with the shy, bucktoothed Muskrat and learn along with him that sometimes we must throw ourselves into the mystery of the spiritual life out of concern for the next seven generations, without regard to personal safety. It is a hero's journey. In the Huron story "The Making of the World," we equally identify with the good brother Tijuskeha, who must endure long years of suffering at the hands of his brother Tawiskarong so that the story of Creation may continue for future generations.

The Wager for the World

There is a long-standing Native American tradition employing gambling as an alternative to war, in combination with what today we call conflict-resolution techniques,[3] much of which is derived from what the Algonquins call the Way of the Heron. The two most commonly used games for this most sacred activity are the peach pit game and the hand bone game, although the dice game (*pukasawuk* in Delaware) is also used. The hand bone game is used to resolve a war between the animals in chapter 5, " 'Why?' Stories"; the peach pit game is used in "The Chickadee Story" to resolve a war between two brothers; and Jackstraws, Pegs, and a staring contest are used by the animals in "Co-No, the World's Greatest Gambler" to rescue humankind from enslavement.

Variations on the peach pit game are well known to Native Americans under a variety of names, including *guskâeh* (peach stone game) in Mohawk, *hubbub* in Lenape, and *woltest* or *woltestakun* in Mi'kmaq, and it was played thousands of years ago in the Aleutian Islands, where a peach pit platter was found by archaeologists in a cave.[4] However, it is little known to the rest of the world.

In addition to the Huron Creation story told in chapter 1, there is a Mohawk story in which two brothers try to decide the fate of the world through first a peach stone gambling game and then a lacrosse game. When both games end in a draw, the "left-handed brother" resorts to war to decide which of them will dominate.

Guskâeh is played at the midwinter ceremony. The stakes involve fifty beans or white corn kernels, instead of sacred sticks. It is said that at one time the game was played only in the presence of the first Atatadaho, or chair person of the Confederacy of the Five Nations, and that when Mohawks go to the afterlife, they are allowed to play guskâeh for eternity. It is played for the "pleasure of the Creator."

In guskâeh, the sacred game, there are six peach pit stones, burned black on one side and left white on the other. They are thrown up in the air and caught with the platter. If less than five fall with either black or white facing up, there are no points awarded. If five fall with white or black showing, the player wins one point. If all six land showing the same color, the player wins five points. Each point is worth a stick. Two teams play until one team wins all fifty sticks. There are several variations in scoring. I recently received a letter from the Mohawk elder Tom Porter that shared not only the current peach stone game (guskâeh) scores, but the current team standings as well! So the tradition is alive and well.

Why is this game considered to be so spiritual? It is thought within the Native tradition that reality proceeds between the inner and outer worlds, so that our beliefs and expectations affect certain aspects of reality and that reality affects certain aspects of our beliefs. Some say that Creator alone decides who wins and loses the peach pit game, but others say they are "testing their medicine" (developing and measuring their inner power and intuition) when they play. These types of games have been used in recent decades by conflict resolution teams and outdoor educators.

In the seed game *atenaha* (which is a social game) there are eight buttons or disks (cut from elk horns, hickory wood, or similar substance) burned black on one side and left white on the other. Players simply shake the eight buttons in their hand and throw them like dice onto a game board. If fewer than six fall white or black, there are no points; if six fall black or white, the player wins two points; if seven fall black or white, the player wins four points. However, if all eight land with the black side facing up, the player gets twenty points. If all eight are white, the player gets ten points. Each point is worth a stick or kernel or bean, depending on the stakes.

It is difficult to understand how gambling can be related to ritual without understanding the concept of Dream Time. Dream Time is hard to understand but simple to experience, in fleeting moments. What parallels exist in world religion? In the Tibetan Buddhist Tantric Mahamudra practice, we strive to merge our innermost minds with the emptiness of reality itself, so that one cannot be distinguished from the other. It is from this state that the yogis achieve their *siddhi,* or miraculous powers, which can come either as gifts from Creator for those who are saintly, or from Tantric understanding possessed by the adepts. In the Native American context, the same view is held. I refer to it as Dream Walking, a way in which, through devotion to spirit, one can walk between two worlds, the symbolic world of dreams and the world of plain reality, and not become lost.

Certainly, most Tibetans and Native Americans who strive for this state do so without resorting to gambling to "test" it, and not all gamblers are Tantric adepts by any means. But the stories preserve the flavor of a time when such "gambling magic" was practiced. In fact, experiments have been conducted on a regular basis at the Princeton Engineering Anomalies Research laboratory for decades to determine scientifically if certain minds can influence randomly produced numbers, shapes, and patterns. I was part of those experiments, and I recall seeing research that indicated that men showed slightly higher incidence of influencing random events in accordance with their intention. In a separate study, it was shown that women are slightly better at intuitive skills, including long-distance viewing and predicting the future. Women tend to get a bigger effect than men, while men tend to have better control over the direction of their effect. Interestingly, men and women in paired combination were by far the most effective in influencing random events. Meditation in either case was a positive factor. Naturally, such results are disputed.

One of the attractions of gambling to the Native American mystic is the paradoxical tension that arises between the need to maintain a detached, relaxed, and divinely indifferent (Zen-like) frame of mind needed to make the right decisions and influence the roll of the dice in one's favor, and the anxiety or fear as the stakes rise higher and higher. Native philosophy says that, in reality, "men possess nothing," an ancient saying that is in harmony with the Pali Canon of Buddhist scripture. And yet, at the same time, we tend to become attached to our things, even if we believe in the old ways. Some think gambling is about greed, but in Native American culture at least, it is equally about non-attachment—surrendering our possessions to fate. Any experienced gambler knows that the chances of losing in a game of chance are close to equal to those of winning. Spiritually speaking, the house always wins!

Kathryn Gabriel writes:

> No historical period or culture on the globe lacks the means for gambling, and it was often associated with death and rebirth. One Egyptian tomb-painting (c. 3500 B.C.E.) depicts a nobleman in his afterlife playing a dice board game of hounds and jackals. A Sumerian board game was found in a royal cemetery dated to circa 2600 B.C.E. Antelope ankle bones, presumed to have been used as dice, are often found in prehistoric tombs and burial caves around the world, perhaps for afterlife recreation, or so the dead could "re-create" life. Icelandic and Hindu mythology mirror many Native American myths that claim that the gods destroy and recreate the world on a diceboard."[5]

This reminds us that everything—and nothing—in life is up to chance.

In his 1901 report for the Bureau of American Ethnology, entitled *Games of the North American Indians*, Stewart Culin concluded, "In general, games appear to be played ceremonially, as pleasing to the gods, with the object of securing fertility, causing rain, giving and prolonging life, expelling demons, or curing sickness."

Dice were used by the Etruscans (and Native Americans) as oracles, while the peach pit game bears a close resemblance to "throwing the cowry shells," a Native American practice in which a certain number of these shells are tossed and if a majority land a certain way, the answer is yes.

The Winnebago story "Co-No, the World's Greatest Gambler" provides a cautionary tale that shows Native Americans have long been aware of the dark side of the mystic art of gambling, and it is rather dark indeed. It teaches us that gambling can become a trap, and that people with powerful spirits are not necessarily well intentioned and can trap us with their games. For this and other reasons, it is good to know when to call it quits.

In the Natchez story "The Adoption of the Human Race," we see another kind of "wager for the world." In Native American oral tradition, it is said that "everybody has a boss," in other words, each animal or spirit being has another animal or spirit being in nature they answer to. One of the things a shamanic healer or "medicine man" will learn during his or her training is from which spirits to ask permission for clearance regarding ceremony and daily activity at which times. To ask the wrong one at the wrong time would be a sort of gamble; any effrontery or presumption may cause a breakdown in future lines of prayer communication. (In an apocryphal context, it would be like making an angelic invocation to the archangel Metatron, and then, upon his appearance, asking him for a cigarette.) In "The Adoption of the Human Race," the various elemental spirits of the sky all answer to Old Man, who is their father, and who is similar to *Tunkashila* (who reports to *Wakan-Tanka*, the supreme being) in Black Elk's book *The Sacred Pipe*. When the human race appears, there is now something of real value on the face of the earth below, and all the sky beings get greedy. They risk their relationship with their father to ask him for a really big favor: the right to adopt the human race as their own. They are like Jacob and Esau in Genesis, who foolishly vied for their father's blessing. In the end, Old Man has a very polite but firm response to all of them, one that is full of teachings for us all.

The Origins of Fire

Just about every storyteller of every Native American nation has told a tale about the invention of fire. This is because every child in the world who has ever sat by a fire, or has ever watched one being built, has asked the question, "Who invented fire?" Most of the time, we answer, fires were lit from other fires, which were lit from other fires, just as wisdom teachings are passed from generation to generation. But children will immediately see through that and say, "Yes, but who built the *first* fire?"

Of course, the answer is it came from the Thunder Beings, the sky spirits who make the rumblings we call thunder and who send lightning down from the sky. Desert people often speak of them as benefactors who give their energy to the earth so that rain can fall. Others say the Thunder Beings not only do destructive things, but they do them in a counterclockwise manner!

Stories from around the world tell us the first fire came from lightning. Lightning is also the source of fire in the Mi'kmaq Creation tale of Glooskap, the First Man, who prays or "speaks as one with Creator" for warmth and is answered immediately, as a lightning bolt hits a nearby piece of dead wood. In the Ojibway Creation stories, it is the Fire Keeper in the West who brings fire to the people. It is the sun in other stories. In fact, most Native Americans by the beginning of the Woodland Phase, in roughly 1000 B.C.E., carried their own fire-starter kits of pyrites and rhyolite (flint). Struck together, they create a spark that can light tinder fungus or a small, dry pile of kindling. (It is said in Cherokee, "The clash of ideas brings forth the spark of truth.") Flint mines such as the one at Coxsackie, New York, were already centers of population and industry at that time. But long before that, it *had* to have been the Thunder Beings.

Another reason there are so many original fire stories is because fire is one of the most important gifts from Creator. Without it our ancestors would have perished. Fire brings us light and warmth, it cooks our food, it purifies, it can be used to soften copper and to help cut down trees, and it gives us council fires around which great decisions are made. When we watch the flames of a campfire, we can almost see shapes and dream-like images.

In Native country, fire is referred to as "the mouth of God," as offerings are fed into it and disappear, and are transformed into pure energy that can come back in any form to benefit the offerer. In the Vedic tradition, Vishnu says, "I manifest myself as the sacred fire that carries the offerings of men on earth to the gods in heaven."[6]

Among the Mi'kmaq, fire is always considered good, as our Creator is. The Tibetans of the Himalayas also teach that fire is always good. The lamas say there are many beneficial spirit beings that we cannot see, but when we place food or other offerings in the fire, the offering is transformed into another dimension where it can be enjoyed by the spirit beings. The Tibetans frequently perform *mé puja,* or fire ritual. Hindus perform regular *yagna,* or fire rituals, in which offerings are made to *Agni,* the god of fire, the protector of people and their homes. The fire keepers are called a*gni-hotras*. Grains, purified butter, and sandalwood are offered to the fire in a special fireplace called a *kund*. In Vedic practice, a minimum of five priests is required. Hindus perform the *yagni* at marriage and burial ceremonies, thread ceremonies, and during the *vastu shanti* (nature ritual for the honoring of elemental deities) as well. In most Native American traditions there are no priests, per se, and one can do fire ritual alone or with others, and no special fireplace is built. However, the sacred fire is built according to specific traditions, varying from place to place. A fire offering of tobacco or corn is to be expected at marriage and burial ceremonies, at powwows, and in rituals honoring the local elemental spirits and guardians.

The Tibetans have a summer festival similar to a powwow, which is little known outside Tibet. According to Lama Norlha Rinpoche, people in Tibet get together each summer for a cultural ceremony, wearing the finest traditional clothing, to enjoy traditional dances and music. The women dress their hair according to ancient fashions and wear elaborate hats and bring traditional food. Naturally, there are fire ceremonies there too, though not right in the center of the festivities. At the other end of the world, the native people of North America engage in powwows, largely during the summer, which present a similar picture. As in Native powwows, at least some if not all Tibetan dances are considered prayers, and some involve spinning and weaving and evocation of birds and other animals, reminiscent of powwow dancing. The similarities in customs between the Tibetans and the Athabaskan (and to a lesser extent all other Na-Dene speakers, which include Dene, Tlingit, Eyak, Navajo, Apache, and Haida Indians, among others), including the women's hairstyles, are intriguing and may have a recent historical basis. Several books have been written on this transcontinental kinship.

Among European traditions of cultural festivals employing fire, the Ukrainian spring festivals are among the most remarkable. Through group dances, fire ceremonies, rituals for spring, songs, baking of breads, decorating *pysanky* or colored eggs, and offerings, the traditional Ukrainians hope to please nature. On the three nights before Easter, the men and boys of the village light bonfires on hills to purify the land, and token household items are thrown into the blaze. As in Celtic custom, bonfires magically encourage the sun.[7] Candles protect houses from lightning, deter illness, and preserve the crops. An ancient Ukranian song used to be sung in which a landowner is awakened by a swallow who tells him that three guests are coming: the sun, the moon, and the rain. The sun is made of fire, and the sun is the closest thing we can see to the divine nature of Creator. In *The Mishomis Book,* by Ojibway elder Eddie Benton Benaise, the Fire Keeper says to Original Man, "You see, fire is a very special gift from Creator. If you respect it and take care of it, it will take care of you and bring you warmth. But locked up in this goodness is also evil. If you neglect fire or use it in the wrong way, it could destroy the entire Creation!"[8]

Many tribal stories emphasize the importance of respecting fire. Many expert fire keepers have found their eyebrows and other hair singed from working too close to the fire: one more reason to respect its power. One such story that teaches us to respect fire is called "Why Fire Came to the Indians." In this story, Fire was in the custody of the Bears, who guarded it very closely, and even carried it around with them. Only members of the Bear Clan were allowed to use Fire or even approach it. Both humans and four-leggeds had to come and trade valuable furs and food just to gain access to Fire. One day, the Bears put Fire on the ground and went away for a few days to gather acorns. Slowly, Fire started dying and began calling for help. Some of the Alabama tribe heard its call and hurried to its aid. "Feed me!" it said, "I'm starving, and soon I might die!" The people asked Fire what he wanted to eat. "First get me a stick from the north and lay it on Fire. Then find another stick from the west and feed it to Fire. The third stick should be brought from the south and laid on the flame. Then go to the east for another stick. When it is laid down, I will blaze up and come back to life." The people did as they were told, and Fire did come back to life, and was very happy. After the Bears had finished their meal of acorns, they returned to claim Fire. However, Fire said, "I don't know the Bears any longer." This is how Fire went to live with the Alabama people. This story teaches respect for Fire, depicting it somewhat like a wild animal. The message is that if we don't respect Fire, other animals may come and take it from us as well.

In Native American oral tradition, the ancestors were "told" by the things of nature how to use them. Fire told them how to build a fire, tobacco told them how to pray, the pine martin told Glooskap it was okay to hunt and kill him for food, and so forth. Even at the beginning of the twenty-first century, it is common to find Native American women talking to plants, asking them questions about how to best use them medicinally.

One interesting aspect of this story is the emphasis on honoring the four directions while building a fire. I have observed this many times among the Algonquin nation of the Ottawa valley and with the Mi'kmaq of New Brunswick; however, they introduce the four splints in almost opposite order from that given in the previous story, going clockwise instead of counterclockwise, usually starting in the east. In general, the east is the direction of grandfather sun, and therefore of fire, of the soul, and of life. It usually comes first, then the south, then west, and finally north. The attributes of the other three directions vary from village to village. Invariably one will be associated with wind and with birds, with thought and speech, and with the messages that come from the spirit world. This is often "in the south." Another direction will be associated with the grandmothers and the moon, with music, water, the path of the heart, and with giving. This is often "in the west." Another direction will be associated with the physical body and its purification, with the wild animals and their overriding spirits, and with the ancestors and the sweat lodge. This is often "in the north." The Great Spirit is the "father of the four winds," and there are helpers, grandmothers, and grandfathers in each of the four directions, not to mention the four winds themselves, who are intimately associated with the naming of the four directions, and this is why we offer a log to the four directions while building a ceremonial fire.

These are the four cardinal directions that have been known for thousands of years by all. At the equinox, the sun rises due east and sets due west and sits due south at noon; the North Star at midnight is above the horizon at due north. The concepts of east, south, west, and north have always helped hunters find their way through difficult terrain, and the associated spiritual concepts, including the four parts of the self, help all of us find our bearings on the Medicine Wheel of Life. There are three more directions not always associated with fire-making ritual; these are the downward direction of ashes toward Mother Earth, the upward direction of fire and smoke toward Father Sky, and the journey back to the center, which is the invisible and most important direction, where our offerings go.

We find parallels to this in all corners of the world. A recurrent motif found on many pre-Columbian Caribbean Taíno artifacts such as ceramic bowls, stone collars, *duhos* (carved effigy seats), and body stamps is the circle, symbolic of the fifth direction, the invisible central hole that connects the earth to the cosmos. In Tibet, there are the four elements of the four directions and also a fifth element of emptiness, which is at the center. In the Mi'kmaq *mayomi* or ribbon shirt design, the ribbon for the east is red, the ribbon for the south is white, that for the west is yellow, and that for the north is black. The sky ribbon is blue, and the earth ribbon is green, but the ribbon for the seventh and central direction, the heart, is invisible. A Tibetan would understand that perfectly, as this is the direction of emptiness, which lies at the heart of reality in Vajrayana tradition. Tibetans who practice the Mahamudra tradition say that the greatest attainment is to rest in the emptiness of Mahamudra, where mind has no motion.

The Sacred Pipe

The pipe as we know it, with its long stem, elbow, and upturned bowl, is the invention of the Native American, and an offspring of Amerindian spiritual traditions. Anthropologists agree that the various smoking pipes that appear today in many cultures around the world—including Irish, African, Eskimo, and Siberian types—all derived from the first pipe brought back from the Powhatan people by Sir Walter Raleigh in 1586, and the pipes that Father John White brought back from the Roanoke Colony the following year.

This form of pipe was unique in the world at that time. The water pipe—variously known as a ganja in India, a nargile in Turkey, and a hookah in Egypt—may have been developed before 1000 B.C.E., but it is of an entirely different nature than the Native American pipe and related in name only. Today, when someone says, "I smoke a pipe," we think of the Native American form.

That the pipe is highly sacred to most (but not all) Native American traditionalists today is well known to readers of all ages, especially since the publication of *The Sacred Pipe: Black Elk's Accounts of the Seven Rites of the Oglala Sioux* in 1953, three years after the death of Black Elk. The pipe is not just sacred to Black Elk's nation, the Lakota, it is sacred to all Algonkian-, Cherokee-, Iroquois/Haudenosaunee-, Muskegian-, Washo-, and Uto-Aztec-speaking nations, to name a few.

Archaeologists have found that the earliest pipes were tubular stone pipes, without elbow or bowl, and arrived in the northeast between 2000 and 1000 B.C.E. It is thought they were first used to smoke tobacco, and that is still the primary substance smoked today, along with *kinnickinnick,* which is a sacred mixture usually including bearberry (*Arctostaphylos uva-ursi*), red willow (*Salix laevigata*), sweetgrass (*Hierochloe odorata*), and a variety of healing herbs. The Lakota use the term *kinnikinnick* to refer to the dried inner bark of the red alder or red dogwood (*Cornus stolonifera*), which is also called "red willow" by Native Americans and is considered very sacred. Although *Salix laevigata* is medicine because it thins the blood, *Cornus stolonifera* is considered to be "medicine" in a more shamanistic sense. Most traditional Native Americans do not smoke mind-altering substances, which are taboo.

When Giovanni da Verrazzano came to Virginia in 1524, he described Algonquin holy men smoking *tubular* pipes. Statues showing men smoking cigars have been found in Mesoamerica dating back to 1500 B.C.E. The word *cikar* is a Mayan word for "to smoke." The tubular pipe is thought to have originated among the Mayans at this time. However, the oral tradition indicates a much earlier entry for the sacred pipe, and tobacco is said to have played a role in Creation itself among northeastern tribes.

In one Mi'kmaq Creation story, the First Man, Glooskap ("he shapes himself"), sees tobacco growing up from the ground, and asks it what its name is and its purpose. It tells him its name is *temaweh* (tobacco) and that it is a medium of exchange and communication between heaven and earth. There are many ceremonial uses of tobacco, but when it is burned, we see the smoke carry our thoughts and prayers to heaven, and they are answered. The pipe is the primary instrument for burning the tobacco. Puffing the smoke (but not swallowing it) is thought to bring a feeling of peace to the smoker. Swallowing the smoke brings dizziness and possibly hallucinations, as described in Carlos Casteneda's somewhat sensational writings, but this practice is not widespread. The correct smoking of the pipe in the sacred tradition is a graceful, peaceful ceremony in which we speak as one with the Creator, honoring all the directions and thanking the grandmothers and grandfathers.

Tobacco is used among most of the pipe-carrying nations as an offering as well. "Everyone who brings an offering must bear sincere inner feelings of repentance and a desire to draw closer to God." This statement, which is from a Jewish Midrashic text, bears a striking resemblance to how most Native American pipe carriers view the use of tobacco offerings in the Native tradition, although asking for help and forgiveness is more appropriate than "repentance," which is not a familiar term. I have heard many Lakota pipe carriers emphatically plead to *Tunkashila* or "Grandfather" in their prayers that we are "miserable" two-leggeds, that we are unworthy and in need of help, a refrain that Franciscan monks would recognize immediately. According to Tiokasin Ghosthorse, the Lakota pipe carrier is humble but does not pray out of desperation. He prays for greater appreciation of the inherent intelligence in the universe—in other words, to accept things as they are. *Unšika* (*un-shee-ka*) means "pitiful" in Lakota, and *unšimala* (*un-shee-ma-la*) means "I am pitiful," but not in the same way it has come to mean in English. *Unšimala yày oyate wani wachi(n) ču welo* means "Have pity on me. I do this because I want the people (all my relations, all creatures) to live." Such servants of God live simply and wholeheartedly, like the *Hanif* ("the penitent ones"), the tribal people who were an inspiration to the Prophet Muhammad when he founded Islam.

The pipe, however, has taken on individual significance, separate from its function. It has become the most sacred object, and should not be displayed as a souvenir. The stem and bowl should remain separated when not in use, inside a pipe bundle or bag, with a sprig of sage in the empty pipe bowl. Although the traditions of how to honor the pipe properly differ from place to place, most Native Americans today acknowledge the traditions of the Lakota, in some way or another, for whom the *chanupa*, or pipe, is central. The lore surrounding the Lakota pipe begins with the story of White Buffalo Calf Woman, included here.

The buffalo is a sacred animal to many other traditions, from New York to Nevada, but perhaps to a greater extent with the Lakota. Therefore, the white buffalo, which is quite rare, is yet more sacred. There have been several born in the last fifteen years, increasing public interest in the story of White Buffalo Calf Woman.

The version told in this book was written down in 1903 by George A. Dorsey, and published three years later in the *Journal of American Folk Lore*, over a generation earlier than the version told by Black Elk in *The Sacred Pipe,* and it differs in a few details. It seems to be a Dakota, rather than a Lakota, version of the story. I have reprinted the story here word for word, except for parts of White Buffalo Calf Woman's speech, which are taken from the Lakota version published in *The Sacred Pipe.*[9] In later tellings, the second man rapes White Buffalo Calf Woman and dies through unspecified means, but in this story, he "outrages" her in an unspecified way, and is killed by a creeping fog that leaves only his bones.

One aspect of Native American spiritual traditions that often seems strange to Europeans is that Creation is described as an ongoing process. There is no written Bible of Native tradition. Some elders thump their own hearts and say, "This is my Bible!" And some will hold the pipe to their heart and say the same thing, without any disrespect toward the King James edition, which they may know backward and forward. If the Bible is a bridge and a medium of communication between humans and God for Christians and Jews, the pipe fills a similar consecrated role for Native Americans. There are no set words connected to the pipe; no true pipe has ever borne an inscription. It does not belong to humankind. The elders say, "I do not carry the pipe, the pipe carries me."

These same elders may say to a priest, "You can't find God in a book. My Priest, my Medicine Man, is up there," and point to the heavens, a metaphorical way of speaking of God, the Great Mystery. In most native languages, there is no word for time, and so everything is here and now, which is a powerful way to live.

This means that we are walking in the days of the prophecies, and that every day is sacred. So when the reader is told, as in chapter 4, that "Yellow Hair" George Armstrong Custer smoked White Buffalo Calf Woman's pipe, and that it still exists today, they may become incredulous. For those foreign to Dream Time, this here-and-now quality of prophecy, constantly adding to the story of the pipe and its people, diminishes the sacredness, because they are sadly convinced that anything of any spiritual value happened thousands of years ago. Traditional Natives, who tend to believe in what they see with their own eyes rather than in that which must be taken on faith, find this view hard to fathom. Even within Christianity, we find that the Mormons faced persecution on their trek westward simply because they believed in latterday saints and prophets and that miracles still occurred in their midst.

Some strangers to Native teachings think that any association with the mundane facts of life makes a mockery of the sacred, when in fact it proves that God is real, and that all life is holy. Therefore the appearance of many white buffalo calves in the last decade is not surprising to many Native Americans. The elders say, "That's how it works."

Since the nature of Spirit is to constantly reveal new and greater truths, sometimes "miracles" and "revelations" are necessary. Although pipe carriers are humble as a rule, it is not blasphemous for one to repeat a message from God imparted directly to the narrator while smoking the pipe, or while fasting or in the sweat lodge. When the pipe is awakened in the proper manner, it becomes a two-way intercom device for communication with the spirit world. Some Jewish mystics hold that the Ark of the Covenant was once used in a similar way. However, the spiritual teaching of ancient peoples was that if you keep your life pure and simple, you will hear and converse with God, without need of priest or temple or any device. Isaiah 58 makes this clear: "Then you shall call and the Lord will answer, you shall cry for help and he will say: Here I am!" In the Native view, the day that Creator stops speaking to us is the beginning of the end. If our friend stops speaking to us, that is bad enough, but if

God stops speaking, that is the most important friend we could ever lose. In my opinion, it is more likely that humanity will simply stop listening.

The pipe carrier, in most traditions, lives by a code of honor, in which he (and, more and more often, she) is totally absorbed in service, not to the people, but to Spirit for the benefit of all people. A pipe carrier lives as a child of God and "follows the spirit" wherever it leads, following signs, visions, and dreams, step by step. Pipe carriers consecrate themselves to Spirit by letting their hair grow, by abstaining from all alcohol, and by trusting the Great Medicine and not soliciting directly for any purpose. They take whatever jobs, goods, or money are offered. They are "the tool of the Creator," but if a job is unethical or unwise, they have the right to refuse it.

The pipe carrier is thankful for absolutely everything, even that which seems "bad." Some call Native Americans the "thank you" people, and their spiritual path the "thank you religion," as thanks are given on every occasion and marked with gifts, feasts, and ceremonies. This was not at all uncommon in early Christian communities: Paul reminds us in Colossians 3:15 to be thankful, but the teaching dates back to Mosaic times. In Deuteronomy 8:10 Moses says, "When you eat and are satisfied, you are to *bless* God for giving sustenance." The Midrash directs us to "Bless even for the volume of an olive or an egg," where *bless* is interpreted as "thank." This implies that if the Jews are the Chosen People, it is to the extent that they are thankful to God and adhere to their original instructions. It comes as no surprise that many Native Americans also see their race as "chosen people," but also only to the extent that they are truly thankful and adhere to their original instructions.

A pipe carrier is expected to fast several times a year, as suggested by the elders, or as inspired by God or by events. Fasting is almost universal among world religions. It is essential to Yoga in India, to Buddhism in Tibet, to the Christian faithful during Lent, and it is frequently mentioned in the Torah, although the Day of Atonement is the only scheduled day of fasting in the Torah. All other fasts in the Jewish tradition are in response to events, which is very Native American. There are no holidays in the Native world, although some lodges meet two times a year.

The candidate for pipe carrier consecrates (dedicates to a sacred purpose) his or her life by fasting alone in the mountains. Some say, "I am going up on the hill," which means they will fast and undergo a "vision quest." The candidate is expected to grow his or her hair long (in most traditions), and wear it either loose or bound up in a pony tail. It is said that Manitou (Great Spirit, Great Mystery, or God in Algonkian tongues) intended our hair to grow long, and to cut it is to go against nature. Nature is the visible Creation of God's handiwork, and a source of wisdom. Children, both boys and girls, raised in traditional Lakota homes have long hair, sometimes woven into three braids. Long hair helps us to "remember where we come from"—which is from the mother.

The samurai warrior in Japan grows his hair long, tied above his head in a topknot. If his hair is cut, it is in humiliation. To find parallels in biblical traditions, you have to go to the Nazirites, whose ways, including the practice of growing the hair long, are explained in the book of Numbers, chapter 6. Samson was a Nazirite whose strength, in part, depended on his uncut hair. Moses says of the Nazirites (which means "to be separated"), "They shall be holy, they shall let the locks of the head grow long."

The Nazirites consecrated themselves for thirty days (or more), during which time they drank no wine or grape products and avoided touching a corpse. It is said in the Midrashic texts that "hair is the body's insulation against the outside world, so that every action can be devoted to God." In Numbers it states, "He is Holy to Hashem (Great Merciful One). The Crown of his God is upon his head." A chief may wear the buckhorns, and a holy man may wear his hair long in all its natural splendor, to express the sacredness of his life. He will drink no wine, not just for thirty days, but for all the days of his life as long as he holds the pipe, and will act only in service to others. Hair comes from the head and is associated with deep thought and also with the "wild" reptilian brain which perceives the world through the entire body. In Robert Bly's words, "Hair is intuition."[10]

The sermon on the Mount of Olives is rich with passages that reveal a profound reverence for nature. If Jesus seems a little "Native American" in some respects, it is perhaps because he was following the indigenous Middle Eastern tradition of the Nazirites, possibly as a reformer of the Essenes, as was John, who wore camel-hair robes (and animal skins) and ate "locusts and honey," separating himself from others by living in a cave. Nazarean Nazirite Essenes had long, uncut hair, which is perhaps why Jesus and John have traditionally been depicted with long hair. The image on the Shroud of Turin suggests long hair.

The pipe carrier's vow is not set in stone but comes spontaneously from his or her own heart. In any case, it is similar to the bodhisattva vow. In Buddhism, one version is based on a sixth-century vow by Tien-t'ai Chih-i: "Beings are infinite in number, I vow to liberate them all. The obstructive passions are endless in number, I vow to end them all. The teachings for alleviating the suffering of others are countless, I vow to learn them all. Enlightenment is the supreme achievement, I vow to attain it."[11]

In general, pipe carriers give over their will to God's will and go where they are moved by Spirit, like one of the *Mamawinini* (an Anishinabi word meaning "men who wander nomadically"). They place themselves at the mercy of God. In Matthew 7:21, Jesus states a similar message: "Not everyone who says to me, 'Lord, Lord,' will enter the kingdom of heaven, but only the one who does the will of my Father in heaven." The word *Islam* means "Submission to God's will," and Muslims are "those who submit to God's will." In the Native world, pipe carriers are those who submit to God's will, becoming the "tool of the Creator" similar to the *bhikshus* in Buddhism renounce the world in order to follow the dharma. The pipe carrier renounces attachments to this world, but not the world altogether, becoming "in this world but not of it" (John 17:15–16). If people truly want spiritual assistance and guidance, the pipe carrier can lead a pleasant life, one that is very busy, like the eagle.

"Why?" Stories

Throughout the world there are many varieties of "Just So" stories, such as those of India which Rudyard Kipling made famous. These stories explain how animals acquired their unique features. Many Native Americans call them "Why?" stories, for obvious reasons; they are meant to be retold whenever a child asks "Why?" Of course many of them are just for entertainment, but some carry special messages, or teachings, that may not become clear until the children listening have long been adults. Perhaps while telling their own children the same stories they heard at their mother's knee, it dawns on them what is really being said.

Native Americans have shared hundreds if not thousands of these stories over the millennia, and they can often be examined for hidden layers of spiritual meaning.

"Why the Blackfeet Never Kill Mice" is a "Why?" story explaining why human beings seem to be the dominant species on earth, and why mice don't seem to want power and control. However, on a deeper level, it is really a story about how certain gambling games are used as an alternative to war, specifically the hand bone game.

The hand bone game has been described as the most widely played Native American gambling game in North America. In *Hand Game,* a documentary by Lawrence Johnson, thousands of Native Americans—including members of the Makah, Blackfoot, Flathead, Spokane, Coeur d'Alene, and Crow nations— take to the "hand game trail" each year to compete for winnings. Each nation has a different name for it. The Cree call it *meecheechee-metawaywin (mee-**chee**-chee-met-a-**way**-win).* In British Columbia it is called *takkulli (tak-**kul**-li).* It is also especially popular among the Delaware and the Wichita Sioux.

According to Michael H. Brown, "The bone game is a ritual of personal and group transformation. It arose out of the need for conflict resolution, developed as an alternative to aggression or war. The game was played between disputing elements within a tribe, between disputing tribes or between nations in conflict. The ritual was a contest of spirit, focused within a gambling game. The essential purpose of the ritual was to help players touch, develop, and make explicitly useful their deepest human potential."[12]

Before the game, the warring groups would talk over what they were willing to put up as stakes; the value of their wager was assumed to be commensurate with the seriousness of their desire to win, and so the interaction was further opportunity to discuss the seriousness of their complaints. Then they entered into a "talking feather" ceremony, in which a sacred object such as a feather was passed clockwise around a talking circle. Only the person holding the feather was allowed to speak, and the silence of the others present was considered sacred. Proposals for solution could be made in the talking circle, but they had to be voted on later, with everyone coming to a consensus.

There are two negotiators on each team: a spokesperson and an advisor to the spokesperson, who remains outside of negotiations with the opposite team. The negotiators help the two teams decide what they are willing to gamble.

The game itself involves four carved bones, or sticks, small enough to hide in the fist of the hand. Two are plain and are called "worthless," and two are ornately carved and painted, and are each worth one point, according to one system of scoring. In another system, every wrong guess costs you a point, while every correct guess earns you a point. So if you find one carved bone and not the other, there are no points, whereas if you locate the two painted bones plus the two unpainted bones, you get four points.

There are two players on each team called "hiders," and they decide which hands to hold the carved bones in. In the contest, they stand side by side. Each player holds one carved bone and one plain, with the carved bones in either both left hands, both right hands, the outside hands, or the inside hands. Each team has a pointer as well. The pointer must access all their inner resources, connectivity, intuition, "good karma," and good graces of Creator, in order to "know" which two of the four hands holds the carved bones. The pointer uses silent hand signals (difficult to describe in writing), which can be performed with one hand, to indicate exactly where the pointer believes the two bones to be. Without divine help, the pointer's chances of identifying the location of both bones is one in four, but a good pointer can often find them several times in a row. The opposing team uses a drum and "chatter," similar to that used in baseball to distract the batter, in an effort to break the concentration of the pointer. There are also hand game songs; some of the music notation for the Salish hand bone game songs have been published online. The first team to accumulate seven points is the winner. In ancient times, this allowed two tribes or nations to resolve their differences without loss of life.

In the story "Why the Blackfeet Never Kill Mice," the stakes are high; the winner will become the dominant species on earth. The game will end the war between the animals. Mouse is the most intuitive and the most attentive to detail of all the animals, and so Mouse wins in the long run, with a surprising twist at the end.

"Why?" stories can be changed slightly to suit the moment, and so I have retold these in my own voice. In Algonquin tradition, parents don't read stories from books—they either make up their own stories on the spur of the moment, usually appealing to the interests of the individual child, or they tell stories they heard as a child, or a combination of the two. Both variations have a freshness and spontaneity that appeals to Native children, especially if they are good children's stories to begin with. Each child will have their own favorites, which they will ask for again and again and again, and those are the stories they will probably pass down to the next generation. I was told similar stories as a child, and made up a few of my own and wrote them down when I was seven. A Ramapough/Cherokee storyteller and good friend, Talking Leaves, made up some rather good "Why?" stories, and he told them along with the ones that are quite ancient.

The Sacred Hero

The myth of the hero has developed through many stages since the beginning of storytelling's long history. In the earliest tales, we find not a warrior hero, but a humble man or woman who uses prayer, magic, and cunning to meet and defeat seemingly unmatchable destructive forces that have set upon their village. It is only during the later agricultural phase of civilization that we begin to see the warrior or defender using brute force in the stories, and later still, after thousands more years of storytelling, that we see a hero who goes out seeking to uncover and combat evil. In the tale of Agulabemu, the great bullfrog who steals all the water in the world, Glooskap goes out seeking the frog only because the people begged him to, so that they would not die of thirst. He doesn't kill the frog but, by transforming himself, he becomes so large he can hold Agulabemu in his hand and squeeze him until he is small.

In my understanding, *Agulabemu* means "without truth or wisdom"; *mu* is "without," and *agula* is short for *agulamz,* a Mi'kmaq word that is hard to define in English, but is quite similar to the Chinese word *Tao.* People interpret agulamz as "the truth of things," "the right way to do things," but add that anything you say about agulamz can only be a part of it. It is indefinable. I have been told, "You can't learn about agulamz from someone else, you have to live it." It is also associated with the Red Road, which is the "path of beauty": a harmonious way of living that connects us with the invisible power of the universe, with the wisdom of nature, and with each other in brother- and sisterhood. It is said of the Tao—literally "the path" in Old Chinese—that "the Tao that can be spoken of is not the Tao." Then it is said that it can be understood on three levels: as the way of eternity, the way of nature, and the way that humankind should live. This is almost identical to agulamz, in my understanding. It is said that to walk that path you cultivate *wu wei*, or nonaction, in order not to disturb that which is already in harmony with the Tao. Even when it is time to act, in order to right a wrong, for example, the sacred hero must act with a sense of *wei-wu-wei*, which is "acting without acting." This is precisely what is meant by the Native American saying "Enjoy life's journey but leave no tracks." Yes, it is difficult, and it's getting harder, but the spiritual benefits are many.

In Cherokee, the word *do* is an everyday word for "good," such as in the expression *wadoh* (wa-**doh**), which means "good, thanks," or *don-*

ada (do-na-**da**), which means "good-bye." I have been told by Cherokee language instructor Brian Wilkes that the variant dohi is a spiritual
term like Tao, with many layers of meaning. Most Native American languages would presumably have such a word. Black Elk, in The Sacred
Pipe, speaks of the Red Road as the north-south cross of the Medicine
Wheel, and the east-west cross as the black or blue road, the way we
should not walk. The Hopi also speak of the good red road and the unwise
black road that leads us down the path to total destruction, such as they
believe has happened three times before to the people of earth.

In J.R.R. Tolkien's classic trilogy The Lord of the Rings, most of the
characters rely on weapons, magic, and athletic heroics to fight the forces
of darkness, but Frodo—the unlikely hero of the story—overcomes evil by
relying more on his wits and pure heart than on his sword, Sting. In the
Bhagavad Gita, Arjuna chose to practice the skills of the warrior, but he
also chose to pray. In the Hebrew scriptures, Moses led the Israelites into
battle, but it was his prayers that parted the Red Sea. The ultimate hero
in spiritual literature is the one who uses the power of prayer to defeat
(or better yet, enlighten) an enemy. The Lord Buddha is such a hero. In
Native American culture, to pray is to "speak as one with Creator" (alsu-
tomai geezoolgh, in Mi'kmaq) and to hear the voice of God whispering
in your right ear, giving you proper instructions on how to help the people. In such prayer, one would expect the gentler creatures of the natural
world to respond to the pleas of the praying hero, and, of course, they do,
as what is nature but the direct creation of the Great Mystery? On a hot,
sunny afternoon in India, when the baby Krishna asks the sun's shadow to
stand still so he may remain in the tree's cool shadow, the shadow agrees,
as the sun is but a reflection of God.

The Native American hero's journey is a magical journey, but sometimes the line between ethical and unethical may become fuzzy, depending on the situation. This is typical of Native American stories, but not
teachings; one is supposed to use these stories as springboards for ethical debate. Plato knew and retold the stories of the Greek gods, who were

anything but ethical, and yet he understood justice as few have since. If the ambiguity were not there, there would be nothing to debate! Native stories challenge us to reexamine our prejudices; of their own hero's journey, the Anishinabi say, "Today I must fight and conquer my greatest enemy—myself!" In the Mi'kmaq stories that pit the culture hero Glooskap against his "evil" brother Malsum, we cheer for Glooskap, but are reminded that *Malsum* means "he is related to you by blood." In some stories, the hero must bend the rules to overcome the enemy, but through prayer is able to make things right again.

The Hopi are traditionally nonviolent people. The name Hopi means "good peaceful people." Therefore, it is not surprising that in the Hopi story "Son of Light Defeats the Monster," we have an example of a real Native American hero: a man who overcomes terrible evil without using violence, transforming the monster with the power of nature, using drastic means only when all other methods have failed, only to find that he hasn't destroyed the enemy but has assisted in his transformation.

Monsters are first and foremost antagonists for the hero to struggle against. The stock villain is just a foil for the main character, but the multidimensional villain is an elemental force of nature that has been turned to the dark side by the evil of humanity in general. The giant frog is a destructive variant on the "serpent" or primordial water being, who in early stories is usually helpful to those who are just and who follow the right path in life, not unlike the four water dragons of Chinese legends, who save the people during a drought. In the same way, Man-Eagle is the fatherly master of the sky powers, turned to the dark side by some unknown conflict. There is a unique, fantastical quality about the Hopi hero tales that may remind some readers of superhero comic books. This is not an accident.

A young artist named Jack Kirby, born in 1917, grew up with an enduring fascination with world mythology and with comics. Kirby was especially interested in the Hopi, and imitated Hopi designs and patterns in his drawing style. Over time, he became known as "King of the Comics," and his enduring interest in ancient Hopi myths influenced millions. Kirby's most personal work of genius, the unfinished "Four Worlds" series, was based on the Hopi myth of Creation by the same name. One can also see his devotion to the Hopi in the creation of his Terrible Totem villain, a wooden character that is an amalgam of several Hopi *katchinas* and monsters. At that time, comic book story writers saw themselves as part of a tradition of heroic fiction, and so did not usually extract whole-sale from existing myths but used elements creatively according to their particular genius. This was the way in which Jack Kirby brought the spirit of the Hopi hero myths to millions of young Americans in the 1950s and 1960s during a time in which people were struggling to find more earth-friendly values.

Jack Kirby (with Stan Lee) invented Spiderman, who embodies many of the qualities of Grandmother Spider, also known as Spider Woman. Kirby and Lee also invented X-Men, whose original characters included The Beast (the forerunner of Beast Boy, a shape-shifter based on Hopi mythology), Ice Man (somewhat like the North Wind of Ojibway stories), Marvel Girl (who is telepathic, and can "talk in someone's ear" without being seen, but in a different way than Spider Woman can), and the Cyclops (from Greek myth). Later X-Men included Mystique, who is a shape shifter. Kirby then invented the Incredible Hulk, who is perhaps like Man-Eagle in many respects, only good. Then he created the Fantastic Four, an arch-enemy of whom was called Mole Man. Unlike the helpful Mole Man in "Son of Light Defeats the Monster," this one is a subterranean menace who controls and unleashes huge monsters upon the Fantastic Four. The Four include the Thing, a rock creature not unlike the Dene (Navajo) Rock Monster Eagle, *Tsé nináhálééh,* who lives on Shiprock Mountain; Mr. Fantastic, who stretches; Invisible Girl, essentially like Grandmother Spider who makes herself so small she becomes invisible; and the Human Torch, similar to the Kokosori Zuni fire katchina who descends from the hills to start the Zuni ceremony of *shalako* on the first week of December. Perhaps contact with these characters has opened our subconscious minds to the teachings of the Hopi, the Peaceful People.

The Return of the Sun

Among all the things we can see in nature, none comes closer to representing the power and vitality of Creator than the sun. Much true Native American storytelling goes on either in the dead of winter when the sun is scarcely seen and greatly missed, or late at night when the sun is not visible. At these times, stories about the tragic loss of the sun, due to some accident or evil being, seem strikingly relevant, and even threatening, as there is a certain hungering for sunlight deep in our bodies after only a short time without it.

There is a whole class of beautiful stories in which the sun either arrives for the first time or is freed from some pit, prison, or net, or is freed from exile in an outer world. Stories benefit from having a happy ending, and what could be a happier outcome than the establishment of light over darkness? In chapter 7 there are versions of three short tales of the return of the sun: "Chipmunk Asks for the Light," "Little Brother Gets Mad at the Sun," and "Raven."

The first is a Seneca version of a story about the arrival of the sun, and how Chipmunk, the four-legged messenger of the forest, played an important role in bringing light to the animals. I like this story because my name *Abachbahametch* in Mi'kmaq means "chipmunk." In fact, the word *chipmunk* is mistakenly based on the Ojibway word for "red squirrels," the plural of which is *ajidamoog (a-**djit**-a-**moogk**)*. The correct Ojibway word for *chipmunk* is *agongos*. The story is set in the early spring, when the chipmunk comes out and sings his song.

The second story, "Little Brother Gets Mad at the Sun," is about winter solstice, a time of year filled with meaning for humankind since the beginning of human history. In Celtic lore, this moment is called "The Victory of the Night," in which darkness, hatred, and fear win out over light, love, and courage. It is imperative that at this most difficult time people band together as one and help each other, praying that the sun will return. In Celtic stories, it is the time when the seed of the child of light is planted, and then disappears or is captured and is not seen again until spring.

In this Winnebago story, the little brother, who has what Freud would later call a Napoleon complex, is filled with the human frailties the Mi'kmaq call *loowaywoodee* (*loo-**way**-woo-**dee***), "bad things in my heart"—confusion, anger, fear, violence. He is the "crippled midget" of Nietzsche's work who possesses no nobility of heart and secretly resents those who do. He is afraid of what winter and the forces of nature will do and wants control of nature—usually a bad idea in Native American tales. His snaring of the ultimate source of life, the sun, is the epitome of evil winning over good. In the eyes of Native elders, the damming of rivers, the harnessing of the atom, and the depletion of the ozone layer are all "snarings of the sun" in various guises, all with equally damaging results. It is completely within the spirit of Native American rhetoric to say, "The sky does not belong to us; we belong to the sky."

The third story, called "Raven," is from the far north and is a very famous story that comes in many varieties. Raven, a cultural hero like Glooskap, is a shape-shifting trickster who can bring gifts or wreak havoc for humankind. Like Coyote, he represents the unruly and ever-changing forces of nature on which humanity depends. Raven is associated with fire in both this and the Cherokee "The First Fire" story, as he is in Celtic lore, due to his color. This story also begins at winter solstice, at the coldest, darkest time of year.

This telling is based on a version from Kodiak Island, but it is found in various forms throughout the Northwest. It contains aspects of many other stories in this book; Sky Chief is similar to the sun father of the heroic twins, whose grandmother is Spider Woman. Raven volunteers, as does Muskrat in "The Mud Diver Story," for a nearly impossible mission that others have failed at. Also like Muskrat, he is laughed at for his efforts, yet succeeds.

Coyotes and Other Tricksters

According to the Washo (pronounced **wa-shiw** meaning "the people") every human being has a little Coyote in them. These stories always use

Coyote (or Weasel) to represent the opposite of everything they are trying to teach, so that the people can learn without being preached to. They
can teach the positive sides of life with Coyote, too, for he can be kind
when he has a mind to, but he is always howling and jumping around and
burning off energy. Coyote represents untamed wild forces, both human
and natural. To lead a good life, you need to be wary of danger, and
Coyote personifies everyday dangers as well as a few extraordinary ones.

Little Weasel is the younger brother of Coyote. Which one is worse?
It depends on what nation is telling the story. You can imagine free-wheel-
ing Weasel and Coyote traveling the countryside, and all the trouble they
can get into. It's usually funny. Sometimes Weasel is so foolish, he brings
out the "big brother" wisdom in Coyote, who must put things back in
order, not a comfortable role for him.

First Light, a Washo storyteller whose name in her language is Dashiw
Wat-le (**Dash**-way **Wet**-ley) told me, "Coyote is not all bad; he was here
before humans. He is a teacher. In almost all those stories, he teaches us
about our actions and how there are consequences to be paid for wrong
actions. He is always learning, but he is also stubborn. He is helping to
teach the younger ones, so that through these stories they can beware
of dangerous situations."

"I heard and saw coyotes out there in the desert," she went on to
explain. "I was there at a gathering at a certain lake, recently in Nevada.
People started drumming and singing and round dancing, and all of a sudden the coyotes started trying to out-sing us. They were getting us to sing
louder and louder. How loud they were! And the coyotes started hooting
and hollering, making noise. I thought to myself, they haven't heard these
songs in a while. They had come to help us along, to encourage us." In
the Washo way of life, the coyote is not a "power animal" because power
animals need to be trusted to be invoked and worked with as allies. The
Coyote spirit is not any more trustworthy than the animal itself.

This chapter also features the stories of a great American storyteller,
Chief Eaglewing. His stories are presented as traditional tales of the Kla-

math River valley, but each also possess a certain artistry of storytelling that gives him a unique but authentic voice. These happen to be trickster tales. In certain contexts, you see the emergence of the individual Native American as artist; in others you see a group statement, an expression of an entire culture. The line is blurry sometimes: Is highly stylized graffiti art, found so frequently in urban areas, a product of a subculture or of an individual? Is a blues jam an individual creation or is it an expression of blues traditions? The same question could be asked of innovative Native storytellers and singers, although it's much more complicated. The Washo Coyote stories included here have been shared and passed down for generations. On the other hand, archaeologists point out that a thousand or so years ago, there was a "school" of proto-Algonquin pottery in which each pot was made as an individualistic art form, no two pots exactly alike, and each with a certain degree of expression and even artist recognition. Proto-Iroquoian pottery of the same era was apparently much more uniform, the product of a collective tribal aesthetic. Today, there is an Iroquois Stone Sculpture school that is highly recognizable and also individual. Chief Eaglewing's stories were told in the individualistic creative spirit of those unknown Algonquin women and of today's famed Iroquois stonecarvers; they bear the thumbprint of an artist at work.

Many of the stories in this book have tricksters in starring roles. What makes these stories stand out are their insights into both human and animal nature and their ability to illustrate both with a single character.

Nature Spirits, Landkeepers, and Tribal Guardians

Native American stories are filled with nature spirits, some of which are not exactly like anything in European folk literature. In some cases, they protect the tribe's surroundings from harm, guarding the natural resources and the people themselves. The Water Babies are perhaps the most sacred beings in Washo stories. The Water Babies, called *Me-tsung* (**Mee**-*sang*) in the Washo language, are ancient guardians of Lake Tahoe (pronounced **Da-ow** in Washo—the white people mispronounced *Da-ow* as *Tahoe* which gave the lake its name in English) and are landkeepers of the area. They are not human, but are powerful supernatural beings. They range up to two feet in height and can change size at will. They disguise themselves when not in the water, but may resemble fish when swimming under the surface and often develop fins. They have long yellow or red hair and sometimes are seen with white chalky skin which can change color. They are generally seen by Washo Indian Doctors (called *Damomlee* [**Da**-*ma-lee*] in Washo, similar to Medicine Man or Woman) and then only occasionally, but such a man or woman will be protected by them. Those who do harm to them or their habitat, or intrude where they are not welcome, or fail to make the proper offerings or sing the proper songs, may be punished. Some believe that those who make contact with them who are unprepared will soon be taken into the spirit world and will not return. This is parallel in some ways to the Eastern Woodland people's regard for owls, who are intermediaries between the land of the dead and of the living. There is some disagreement as to whether owls are only capable of bringing omens of death, or bring death itself. Water Babies earn even more respect than owls.

Enter the classic trickster characters Coyote and Weasel (Coyote is called *Damollale* [*Da*-**mol**-*la-lee*], and Weasel is called *Pawetsile* [*Pa*-**wet**-*sol-lee*]) parodying shortsighted human greed and bumbling duplicity in contrast to the graceful power and sacredness of the Water Babies. Coyote and Weasel were among the first creations of Old Man, the Creator. Their story is similar to the story told among the Melanesians of New Britain of how the First Man drew a picture of two men, who became the two tricksters *To Kabinana* and *To Karvuvu*. To Kabinana draws a fish and brings it to life; To Karvuvu tries to imitate his brother and accidentally creates a man-eating shark.[13] Such it is with Coyote and Weasel. In the Washo story, Weasel is also an incompetent sidekick to the demigod Coyote, and true to the "Why?" story tradition, we learn how the familiar bodies of water in the Washo region got so far inland, formed by Weasel's foolish disrespect for the power of the Meesang.[14]

Coyote existed long before humans were on the earth. According to storyteller First Light, Bear was the one who wanted to make the Washo people. If he sat by the water at Lake Tahoe, he could create new beings out of the clay. Coyote said, "I'll help you." Bear said, "No thanks, I know what to do!" So the benevolent Bear made wonderful beings he called "humans" out of clay. Short-tempered Coyote was miffed. These clay figures were the first "earth people," made out of the earth itself, and he didn't get to have a part in it.

These new beings, "human beings," Bear called them, were strong—strong legs and arms and big shoulders in Bear's own image. After he fashioned them out of the earth, he put them in the sun to bake. He left them out in the sun too long and they became too dark. So he made more. He pulled them out of the sun before they burned, but they came out too light. Making human beings was hard work.

Coyote was in the background the whole time, teasing Bear relentlessly, saying, "They are so dark, they look like ravens. If you're making ravens you should at least give them wings!" Or, "That new batch, they are so pale." Bear was so discouraged by what Coyote said, he let the people walk away, and they became neighboring native bands, explaining the variety of skin tones in the region.

By the third time, Bear knew how long to leave them in the sun, and they came out just right. These were the Washo people, of course. At the very moment Bear was finished standing his "people" upright and saying, "Look what I did! Look at my creation!" Coyote ran as fast as he could, and, coming from a distance, he tripped Bear, knocking all the Washo people down. Bear got up again and started putting the people together again, but they were broken into pieces. Some of the pieces of the legs were lost in the confusion.

Bear patched everything together, but he never found those leg pieces. The elders say, "We Washo lost a little length in our legs. That's why many of the Washo people have short legs today!" In this story we can see how Bear and Coyote represent untamed forces of nature and how they affect the lives of humankind.

In a related story about nature spirits, when Creator was bringing down the seeds of the humans, he had them divided up into his different regions. But West Wind was watching and said, "What is this Being doing, gathering seeds, and making piles, and looking down on the earth?" When Creator had the seeds in their different locations and was ready to bring them down to earth, the mischievous West Wind blew as hard as he could, and scattered the seeds eastward. The Washo people are from the West, and they say that "a lot of our seeds were blown into the Great Plains and became the Great Plains people, and that's why the Washo are not a big tribe, because of the mischievous West Wind."

The Washo also have a number of monster stories that serve various purposes besides being good fireside entertainment. Among the most popular are stories about one of the biggest monsters of all, *Hanuhwui-wui* (*Ha-na-**wee**-wee*) who had the power to make the people black out when they heard his *wee-wee* call, and then devour them. Another is about *Mashaygo*, a mean spirit whose very mention inspires children to stay inside at night. Many Washo today, including First Light herself, grew up hearing the words, "Don't go outside, you might see Mashaygo!"

The Great *Ong* (sometimes spelled Ang) is a monster bird of Washo lore that used to sit atop a high tree in the middle of the lake, overlooking Lake Tahoe. It is similar to a number of giant man-eating birds in stories told in Indian country (including Man-Eagle of the Hopi). In Cree legends it is called *Piyesiw*, in Illinois language it is *Piasa*, in Pawnee, *Hu-Huk*. In each case it is killed with poison arrows, as in the Washo story. Other world cultures have their monstrous man-eating birds as well. Herakles drove the horrible *Ornithes Stymphalides* from Lake Stymphalis in Arcadia. In the Fiji Islands, the creature is called *Ngani-Batu*. Then, of course, there was Prometheus and his giant eagle. In "The Great Bird Ong" story, we see how this pterodactyl-like creature works as a foil to bring out the resourceful heroism of the main human character. The story is also an example of the Native American fantasy genre, although the Washo say they remember back to the time of the giant birds, and even the descendants of the pterodactl, through their storytelling. The Ong story is interesting because it is consistent with the Washo view of their landscape: huge, powerful, awe-inspiring, and not to be toyed with. It teaches the listener to respect not only the power of the Me-tsung but of the other creatures as well.

The line between reality and fiction is different in Washo storytelling. Sometimes conventional people "down the street" interact with super beings, monsters, and fantastic creatures, and some live to tell their tale (some don't). Bible stories often mix fantastic supernatural events with real history, and we suspend judgment because it happened so long ago; the parting of the Red Sea is an example. But the Washo, like many Native American nations that hold to traditional beliefs, tell similar stories as if they happened last week, not three thousand years ago, which disturbs some people. But the Washo are living in biblical times, by their standards, though little of it is written down. In Native American spirituality, if you are living right, according to your original instructions for *your* people, and you love Creator, whatever you call him (or her) in your belief system, then you are part of the continuing work of Creation. In some of the stories of the mountain ancestors, the Me-tsung reveal themselves to those who are willing to do the work of Creator, to help Creation continue. But when gifted the right songs and guided by the right energies, then we too can awaken and assist the Me-tsung in their efforts to preserve the land and water (which are presently in peril) and their ancient people. No one knows who will be acknowledged by the Me-tsung, but it is usually those with a strong sense of purpose and intention.

Welekushkush (Wel-ley-kush-kush) was one of the greatest of the Washo doctors (as they refer to medicine men) and would go to Cave Rock and stay as long as he needed. To go to Cave Rock, according to tradition, there are requirements: you need to have the vision, you need the permission, and you need to have the song. He had all of these. The people could tell that he had been changed by the experience. People said the Water Babies communicated with him.

It so happened that he was at Lake Tahoe when a little boy drowned. Welekushkush took his rattle and started singing. He walked straight into the water, disappeared beneath the surface, and was under there for ten minutes. He retrieved the drowned boy and appeared again, walking out of the lake with the boy in his arms. He brought this boy back ashore, and doctored him, and the boy started breathing. No one could believe it. He said he had learned the ways from the Water Babies at Cave Rock, and that one of the Water Babies was his guardian. When he started singing their song, he was able to go to speak to the king of all the Water Babies and he negotiated with the king for the life of the boy. Because he had been so helpful with his songs and offerings, they granted his request.

Hundreds of years ago, Slide Mountain, which was part of Mount Rose in the Carson Valley, collapsed during an earthquake. There was a Washo encampment at the bottom of Mount Rose. There was a large rock slide and many people at the encampment vanished. Today it is taboo for the Washo to visit. We can all see that rock slides are neither good nor bad; they are simply a force of nature that might be avoided if you respect the power of nature and know how to read the signs. Likewise, Water Babies are neither good nor bad, but because they are powerful defenders of the earth, we should avoid harming them, for the earth brings us food, medicine, and everything else we need. The Washo say that the Water Babies can be excellent spirit guides for those who have the gift of vision or hearing and can protect one from all danger.

The Me-tsung can travel wherever there is water, and the Washo believe there are underground channels in Lake Tahoe and caves that lead everywhere.

These types of stories make us open our minds and expand our view of reality. They place us in a world where anything is possible, where the veil between this world and the spirit world occasionally vanishes.

Another Washo monster tale is told something like this: "They say when the sky turns purple, and then orange and red, it's time to bring the children in, because the monsters can come out. Nentusu (**Nin**-ta-

shoo), a respected woman of the tribe, knew her granddaughter was gambling and playing hand games at the meeting place, so when she heard that *wee-wee* sound, she went to warn them, to tell she heard the sound of the monster coming. Of course the young people didn't listen, and grandmother returned home. The young people at the meeting place heard the sound moments later and thought it was grandma fooling them, until the door burst open and Hanuhwuiwui appeared at the door. All the people died and Hanuhwuiwui went searching for others, intending to kill them as well. Grandmother abandoned her home, and ran with the young children (her great-grandchildren, whom she had been watching) into the sage brush, into the area now known as Double Springs Flats. Grandmother found the largest sage bush and spoke with it, and grandmother pulled it out of the ground, which left a big hole. She put the children inside and crawled in after them and pulled the sage bush over them, pulling it by its roots. Then Nentusu twisted her wooden digging stick into the roots and laid the cane across the hole. And then Hanuhwuiwui appeared with his keen senses. He said, "It tastes as if people are right down here!" He pulled on the sage bush, and pulled and pulled but the digging stick at the bottom anchored the roots and he could not pull the sage bush out. Hanuhwuiwui was frustrated and began pulling up all the other sages, clearing an area of five hundred feet around the big sage bush, the only one left in the middle. Hanuhwuiwui tried to catch the old woman by surprise, but she was wise in her ways. After some time, she heard Hanuhwuiwui coming again. She undid her wooden digging stick. When the monster grabbed the sage again he pulled with all his might and it came out easily. He flew back and killed himself on the rocks. That is why she is called Nentusu, as no other grandmother could do that. This is why the sage is sacred. The elder knows best. If she had not known the old ways and not known what plant to ask for help, those children might have been killed."

The native elder or storyteller might mention the names of some locals who disappeared, "Old Man Thompson who lived past that mountain there—he got caught by that monster. Never seen again! You remember young Buck Smith? He had a nasty encounter with that monster. You know that scar on his face? Who do you think gave him that scar?" You get the idea. It scared anthropologists as well as children! Native Americans of all nations used to tell stories like that—and a few still do.

This type of teaching story has survived in the mainstream culture only in the occasional "ghost story," a tradition that was once widespread, but is dying out. In the authentic American "ghost story" tradition, the storyteller is often a character in a fantastic story that brings chills and makes your hair stand on end. Like Sasquatch and alien visitation stories, we never find out if it was really true, and a good storyteller will never deny that it happened just as he described. All the evidence in the world will not convince a nonbeliever, and will not discourage the faithful either.

Why specifically is Cave Rock sacred? Is it because the Water Babies are there? Because the Great Bird Ong was nearby? Is it because it was a place where the ancestors sought shelter? Cave Rock is sacred for all these reasons, but also because when the cannibals attacked the Washo, the Water Babies lured them to the spirit lodge deep within the cave, saving the Washo people. The Washo say, "It is our earth-cathedral and is sacred for the energy it holds."

There is a higher cave on Cave Rock, which is difficult to access. In the early 1980s, rock climbers made forty-seven different trails over the gray volcanic stones of Cave Rock, and placed hundreds of steel footholds or rivets in the rock to make the cave accessible to rock climbers. Worst of all, they placed a cement floor in the bottom of the sacred cave.

Many hundreds of climbers have visited the cave to have picnics and drink alcohol, even though most Washo elders do not feel worthy to enter the cave themselves and must undergo not only purification ritual, but must receive a song such as a Thunder Being song, and other special blessings from the Grandmothers and Grandfathers, before securing safe passage there.

The Washo people have always stated that this one particular rock is a traditional cultural place for them, and that the climbers can climb anywhere else they please. A case brought by a group who wanted access to the cave finally came before a U.S. federal court on January 28, 2005, and the decision was made to ban rock climbing at Cave Rock. The Washo people were grateful. There is now a case in the courts to remove the footholds and metal rivets from the rock and to remove the cement from the cave floor, because the Washo feel it blocks the energy. Further, the Washo would like exclusive access to the cave and to Cave Rock.

Cave Rock is very sacred to them, like Mount Sinai to the Jews, Golgotha or the Mount of Olives to Christians, Deer Park to the Buddhists, or Mecca to the Muslims. My Washo contacts have shared certain information with me about Cave Rock, and encouraged me to publish it for the first time, in hopes that it will impress upon the public that this cave is extremely sacred and not to be visited by the uninitiated. A Washo elder said, "Only about three percent of our entire people have ever been to Cave Rock. That's how sacred it is to us."

These stories and the details surrounding them are not always freely shared with outsiders; however, they are being shared at this time because the Cave Rock case is now being taken to a higher court and is in danger of being overturned. The Washo hope that the informed public will realize the importance of this quest and help them by petitioning the government to restrict access to this sacred area.

The Spiritual Journey

Teaching tales of Native American culture are not always perceived as "spiritual" in the eyes of the modernized mainstream. They often seem quirky and strange, or "too earthy" and "pointless." But the Native tales of the "spirit journey" are easy to recognize, full of fantastic wisdom, elders, and inspiring, uplifting words on the meaning of life and death. Around the world, the words used for soul and spirit are often the same, implying that true spirituality is simply paying attention to the needs of the soul.

In most Algonkian tongues (in this book, "Algonquin" refers to the Algonquin people and culture; "Algonkian" refers to linguistic matters in the Algonkian family of languages), the word for the soul usually is based on the word *tchichan* (think of it as "greater self"). In Ojibway, for example, it is *tchitchaak*. In Mi'kmaq the word for our soul, literally "our shadow soul," is *ootchtchichanhaumitch*, whereas the word for our "blood soul" is *ootchtchichanhaumitch(oo)*. When we face the One Great Sun, our shadow is there and yet not there; it looks like us, but can disappear and reappear at times, just like our spirit body. And like our spirit body, it is sometimes large and sometimes small.

In the teachings about the soul or individual spirit and its relationship to the Great Spirit, it is said that our soul is like a bowl that has been submerged in a great river. We ask the children, "What's the difference between the water inside the bowl and water outside the bowl?" The best answer is, "Nothing, except it's inside the bowl!" It sounds almost like a Zen Buddhist koan, but paradox is just as prevalent in Algonquin culture as in Japanese and Shinto traditions, especially when speaking of that which is both infinite and finite.

The Tibetan Buddhists say that the self is made up of aggregates of consciousness called *skandas*, and that they too are like a shadow; there is no clear line of division between the emptiness or void that is outside the skanda of the self, and the emptiness that is inside the self; indeed, they are the same emptiness. The aggregate self is like a bowl made up of many things—mental constructs that we are clinging to. In the Kagyu Tibetan Buddhist tradition of the Kalachakra Tantra, it is said that before a student takes refuge, she is like a bowl turned upside down: the water of truth will pour off it instead of filling it up. But once she takes refuge, she creates a *tendrel*—an interdependent karmic connection—with the Buddhas and bodhisattvas, and she becomes like a bowl turned upright: the water of truth fills her up. She retains the blessings of the Buddhas and bodhisattvas, and she can proceed on the Path. Nonetheless, the very existence of this "shadow," or bowl, is illusionary as well.

When we break through these barriers of the unenlightened mind, we experience liberation from suffering and from limitations in consciousness.

Similarly, in the Native American context, when we are convinced by others that the world is solid and that nothing invisible to the naked eye exists, no spiritual journey is possible. We become attached to objects in this world. Then something—Creator—opens our hearts and we realize that the invisible is also real. Later we explore our thoughts as real. When we wake up to the spirit world, we become fond of visions, and they become our sustenance, and we turn our back on things of the senses. At the end of the journey, we face the sunrise again and see all as one, this insight awakening in us a greater ability to be used as a "tool of the Creator." Our medicine is strong.

In the Upanishad teachings of India, there is no clear dividing line between Atman, the individual soul (or inner self), and Brahman, the Godhead, the core of all existence (or universal self). Brahman is like a river that flows into the vessel of soul, Atman, from its center and flows out again. Atman is rooted in Brahman.[15] Seen together, they are called Brahmatman.

Likewise, in Algonquin esoteric tradition, we say that the soul is like a stone bowl; it is but a shadow that separates the Great Spirit from our own identity, and yet there is no line at which we can divide God from ourselves and say, "This spirit is God's spirit, and this spirit is our spirit." The waters of life run strong inside of us and outside of us. It's the same water. When we see this bowl or shadow self from "below" we see it as pure white light, but with features. In fact, from the divine perspective, it is but a shadow holding in the light. *Haumitch* refers to this bright shadow. It is the vessel in which we traverse the spiritual oceans *abachtuk,* "way out there somewhere on the ocean." It is literally our white stone canoe, and when we journey at night ("sit in our chair and go somewhere," as the Lenape say), we can visit joyful worlds where there is no pain or suffering. By the way, there actually is a "happy hunting ground" in that world, a sportsman's paradise, so to speak, but it is only one stop on a very great journey.

Frank Setpee, an Anishinabi elder, has had many brushes with death. Although now bound to a wheelchair, he talks to crowds far and wide about the spiritual world to come. He tells them, "The Creator has promised each of us, regardless of religion, that those who are truly seeking will see the light after they pass beyond this earth!" He says they will each be granted the spiritual vision to see their way clear to where they need to go and to fulfill those dreams left unfinished in life. Of this he feels very sure. I suspect if we were to study all the indigenous spiritual paths and read all the religious scriptures of the world, we would find this promise has been given to every nation through different channels and in different ways. This makes me perceive the words "happy hunting ground" in a more universal light.

The last tale in this collection is an Ojibway description of that spiritual journey that takes us beyond the boundaries of death. Like the stone canoe in the story of the Huron Peacemaker, it adds a supernatural element to the narrative, representing the vessel of the soul. This teaching tale shows us that there are many different kinds of landscapes or planes of existence in the world of the dead and that we create much of it ourselves through our fears and expectations. We learn that death, like the last page of a book, is not the end of the journey but the beginning.

1
Creation
Stories

▤ "The Mud Diver Story" was told in the Munsee Delaware language hundreds of years ago and translated into English, the tongue in which it has been shared and loved around the world. This is my own reconstruction of what the Munsee might have been like, based creatively on what I learned from Munsee elder Beulah Timothy and from well-known sources for Munsee language. Munsee is difficult and so I apologize to the Munsee ancestors for any shortcomings. Here, boldface type indicates a stress syllable. The x is guttural, as it is pronounced in Spanish; the n is nasal as in French; and (woo) is not voiced.

This story is one of the most prevalent myths among Native Americans today. The most widespread account of Creation among the pre-Indo-European, Finno-Ugric-language-speaking peoples of ancient Europe is very similar. This strikingly similar variation on "The Mud Diver Story" is still told in the area extending from eastern Finland to the Ob River and in the Volga River area of Russia. It is also well known among the Siberian peoples. Yet another similar story is told by the Ottawa (O-**da**-wa) and other peoples who live near Mackinac Island, Michigan. Loon, Beaver, and Otter fail, but Muskrat succeeds.

1 Most cultures around the world have a flood story, including Native American, which has several. In the Persian story of the flood, ten days of terrible rain was caused by a battle between good and evil and celestial beings, and the resulting floodwaters stood the height of a man over all the earth. This was described in the Bundahis, the Book of Creation of the Zoroastrian faith. In the Bible, the flood was caused by God in order to purify the human race of evil. In the Munsee story, the animals are innocent, and so the nature of the flood is closer to Genesis, which states, "In the beginning, God created the heavens and earth. Now the earth was formless and empty, darkness was over the surface of the deep, and the Spirit of God was hovering over the waters." In Genesis 1:9, God says, "Let the water under the sky be gathered to one place and let dry ground appear." And it was so. God called the dry ground "land." It is a plausible narrative, cosmic forces made graspable by the human mind, whereas "The Mud Diver Story" is full of magic and imagination and things hard to visualize.

☐ The Mud Diver Story (Munsee)

Gu-**tak**-a-**mae**-o **laa**-wa-**tay**
   One day, a long time ago

Kitch-i kwee-**nee**-pay-oo dal-lo-**wee**-ga-man aa-**kee**
   a great, deep water overwhelmed the earth[1]

M'bee a-**boo bwee**-sheh-ye
   The water, it was very deep

Mat-ta ka-**bee**-ha-kee
   There was no dry ground

Ees au-**wa**-sisk men-**no(n)k**-suk
   But the animals were unhappy

Woch **bees**-a-la-ma-**less**-n woo-undj **mat**-ta ka-**bee**
   and they were weak and sickly from not being dry

(continued on page 5)

3

2 *Powwow* did not originally refer to a meeting. That word was *mah-wen* in Munsee. Powwow was the name of a particular holy man, the equivalent of "He dreams," and the sacred gatherings he conducted became large and significant. Soon, sacred gatherings were called pow-wows and, later, nonsacred gatherings as well. Today, in English, pow-wow is used to refer to an important decision-making meeting, which this one was.

3 *Tpoos-ga-oo-wee-aych-ton* is an ancient word meaning "to make it right." This echoes a traditional tenet of the medicine path of Native American spirituality, which is to always seek to restore things to balance as you leave. There is no sin or guilt on the medicine path, but we must repay all debts, resolve all misunderstandings, and fix what is broken before we move on. That is why there are no "Native American Express" credit cards—whenever something is taken, you always give back.

Native people say, "We were never kicked out of the garden of Eden. We still expect this earth to be paradise, which is as Creator intended it. Let's clean it up. Living is an art and we strive to perfect it." A somewhat apocryphal story, told among Native American elders, says that Adam and Eve had neighbors in the Garden of Eden, the Red Hawk family next door. After ousting Adam and Eve, God went to the Red Hawks and said, "You are naked, and are in sin! Get out!" Buddy Red Hawk looked up to heaven and said, "I'm sorry, what did you say? What is this word, 'sin'? We don't have this word in our language!" And God left them alone. In fact, it wasn't exactly in Jesus's language either. In Aramaic, the word for sin is *hamartia,* which means "to miss the mark" as with a bow and arrow. If a Munsee missed the mark, he would simply aim again, *tpoos-ga-oo-wee-aych-ton,* to make it right.

4 *Sh'kwal-and-han-nee* is an interesting word. *Sh'kwal* is any kind of frog, and *andhanni* means "he has big eyes"—in other words, a bull-frog. Although a frog can be a "totem," or power animal of transformation, the bullfrog's descendants often appear in stories as greedy;

*Neek-a-ma-wa **ma**-wee-en Powwow*[2]
>   so they gathered in a meeting

*tpoos-**ga**-oo-wee-**aych**-ton*[3]
>   to make it right.

*(Woo)**shee**-way-oh e-**lay**-nee-**aych**-soo*
>   Duck spoke, saying,

*"Da-lo-way-len-**da**-men a-**sing** a-**wee**-keh gut-**tab** w-**see**-xaay!"*
>   "I would like more than anything to have a place to build a nest!"

*Sh'**kwal**-and-**han**-nee ee-**lay**-nee-aych-soo*[4]
>   Bullfrog spoke, saying,

*"**Da**-lo-way-len-**dam** ha-**kee** a-haa-la-**maaxch'l**."*
>   "I would like more than anything for land to hop around on!"

*Xwashk-**sheesh** e-lay,*
>   Muskrat said,

*"Nee **match**-ay-len-**da**-men a-**sees**-ku-sing **wee**-khe xwashk-**seesh**-wee-**goo**-um!"*
>   "I would love a muddy place to build a muskrat lodge!"

*T'**kwak'**l ee-**lay**,*
>   Painted Turtle said,

*"Mu-**kweeg gee**-la-nook **asch**-o-will look-**haa**-mun m'**bee**-sus*
>   "Why don't we all swim to the floor of the lake

(continued on page 7)

their "eyes are too big for their stomachs." The giant bullfrog Agula-bemu who sucks up all the water so no one else can drink, found in the Mi'kmaq story in chapter 6, is an example of such a greedy bully.

5 The Mordvin people of Estonia and Russia (who speak a language related to Sami) have many stories that are similar to certain Native American stories. In their Earth Diver story, God sits on a rock in the middle of the primeval sea and spits into the water. The saliva begins to grow and God strikes it with a staff, whereupon the devil comes out of it in the form of a goose. God orders the goose to dive into the sea for earth from the bottom. On the third attempt, the goose succeeds but tries to hide some of the earth in his mouth. The Cheyenne, who are Algonquin people like the Munsee, have a similar story. In that story, Maheo, the Creator, is floating on the water. He gathers all the birds that swim together, and asks them to dive to the bottom of the sea to find the clay with which he must make the world. Many try but fail to find the mud. Finally, the coot or mud hen, a small blue duck, dives down and reappears with mud from the ocean bottom in its beak.

6 In the earlier versions of the story, I believe that the mud-diving turtle would have been the Muhlenberg mud turtle or its close relatives. It is one of the most ancient of creatures, somewhat prehistoric looking, the grandfather of the snapping turtle. It is known for diving down to the mud, burrowing under, and coming up with mud on its back. More modern versions always mention the painted turtle, which represents the beauty of the earth as we know it today.

7 *Ah-kink* means "unworthy," and is usually associated with a hand gesture, "to throw down to the ground."

The word is used ironically here, as there was no ground. The place of origin of this story has been identified by John Bierhorst as Bayonne, New Jersey, and from that location, nearby Staten Island appears much like a turtle. That island was once submerged beneath the mammoth lake (now New York Harbor) that was created after the melting of the Wisconsin glacier. As melt-off increased, the water rose and

*woch **a**-mu-il as-**sees**-ku?"*
and raise up some mud?"**5**

***Neek**-a-ma-wa e-**lay**,*
   They said,

"Da-bo, T'**kwak**'l,
   "Okay, Painted Turtle,

***gee aan, nay**-ta-mee-**eh**-hen!"*
you go first!"**6**

So Turtle dived down, but had to turn around and surface before reaching the bottom. Then Duck dived down but had no luck either.
   Frog gave it a try with a high leaping dive, but failed to bring up any mud.
   The animals were disappointed.

*T'**kwak**(oo) (Woo)**shee**-way-oh, woch **Sh'kwal**-and-**han**-ni,*
   Painted Turtle, Duck, and Bullfrog

*ah-**kink**!***7**
   all were unworthy!

*Mo-**hwa** wool-lay!*
   It was no use!

*Met-ta-**len**-sit Xwashk-**sheesh** e-lay,*
   Then, the humble Muskrat said,

*"**Noo**-lee-nu ka-**mee**-lun wee-**tcheen**-gay."*
   "I would like to give you some help!"

(continued on page 9)

broke the natural dam to the south, draining the lake and revealing the "turtle." The Clovis people who were there at the time are among the ancestors of the Munsee, leading us to speculate as to the *real* age of this story.

8 In this story, it is the littlest one who becomes the hero, which is often the way in Native American stories, designed to keep children's attention and to make them feel important. Like many teaching tales, the hero of the story must make a sacrifice for the others, and often gives his life to bring a blessing to the tribe. Humans are often less inclined to make this sacrifice for their families than animals are. It is only because the muskrat gave his life that we have life today on this beautiful continent called *Minsi Tulpehoken,* or Turtle Island.

In a sense, Muskrat was the first Land Keeper. The Land Keepers are the spirits of the dead who choose to stay on Turtle Island to continue as spirit helpers for those who defend Mother Earth. This tradition is still upheld by many nations, including the Mayan, the Hopi, and the Algonquin. Thomas Banyacya, speaking at the United Nations in December 1992, said, "The Traditional Hopi follows the spiritual path that was given to us by Massau'u the Great Spirit. We made a sacred covenant to follow his life plan at all times, which includes the responsibility of taking care of this land and life for his divine purpose.... Our goals are ... to promote the welfare of all living beings and to preserve the world in a natural way."

"The Mud Diver Story" is more than just a Creation story: it implies that we are coworkers with Creation and even though we are too small to be Creators ourselves, Creation, which is still going on right now, can't happen without our help. Co-creation sometimes has its rewards too: The Prophet Muhammad said, "Whoever revives dead land, it shall be his."

9 In the Mordvin version of this story (see note 5 above), while God scatters the sand upon the waters, the dry land begins to grow and the goose's deceit, hiding some dirt in his cheeks to keep for himself, is unmasked. The earth found in his large cheek becomes mountains and hills. In the Cheyenne version, the mud coot places the mud

Woch **nee**-*ka-ma-wa e-lay*
>   And the others said,

*"***Kel**-*la-wak, Xwashk-***sheesh**,
>   "For sure, Muskrat,

Pak-*hee* **gee**-*oh!"*
>   Knock yourself out!"

*Met-ta-***len**-*sit Xwashk-***sheesh**,
>   Poor, humble Muskrat

ahn-*gel-lunk ox-***mpee**-**wah**-*la-***dax**.
>   died during his water journey.

*Ees ox-***teo** *wick-aschk,*
>   But there in his claws,

*ox-***teo** **pto**-*ko-***lin**-*tchees,*
>   in his little fist,

*a-***sees**-*kwol!*
>   was some mud![8]

*(Woo)***shee**-*way-oh, ees* **Sh'kwal** *and-***han**-*ni*
>   Duck and Bullfrog

*Neesk-toon-***hey**-*oh t'***kwak**'*l a-***kee**-*kun.*
>   spread mud on Painted Turtle's back.

*Gut-***tah** **min**-*sees aa-***loo**-*mee-ken.*
>   A little island began to grow.[9]

(continued on page 11)

lovingly in Creator's hands, in service to Creation. Maheo piles the dust of that on the water's surface. The piles grow quickly until they form the continents on which humankind now lives. Note that in each story, though they originate from opposite ends of the Northern Hemisphere, God fashions the dry "sand" or "dust" from wet clay, and then places it on the surface of the water where it forms dry land. This strange and illogical story line has pre-Columbian origins on both sides of the ocean. Some recent theories of history allow for contact between ancient Amerindians and indigenous Caucasians during the last ice age, which would help explain this coincidence. The Mordvins are a very ancient people. Perhaps their ancestors knew the Munsee ancestors! We'll never know.

10 This is not meant to be taken literally, but is suggestive of great earth-building forces.

Ktchi-m'pee a-lum-shee-moo lo-wa-nay-oo
mook-a-mee-kep-al.
>   As the great waters retreated to the ice caps of the north[10]

Min-si Tul-pay-bo-ken aa-loo-mee-ken,
>   Turtle Island grew well, growing wider and wider

nee-gay paa-nay-oo Ktchi-ha-kee a-poo wee-goo-um!
>   until now it is the great land in this certain place where we live!

En-end-hak-keen-day-o Le-na-pay gee-shay-lay.
>   This—this is the Lenape creation story!

1 It is customary when telling Native American stories in English to use terms like "tree people," "rock people," and so on. For example, in Black Elk's foreword to *The Sacred Pipe,* he refers to the birds as "winged people."

2 The opening part of this story is one of the most widespread stories of Creation and is often woven into the Munsee tale given above. Most Iroquoian speakers have a similar story, as do the Lenape. In the Mohawk story, however, the brothers are not judged good and evil; the firstborn is called "the right-handed brother," and the second-born is called "the left-handed brother."

3 "The Falling Woman" ties in with stories from farther west in which a human woman is taken for a wife by a divine sky being. After a few years she forgets about the earth world and is content. One day she pulls up a root and through the hole she sees down onto the earth. She remembers all her relatives and starts crying. She falls down the hole and lands on earth. Her sky husband then must try to find her again and take her back to the sky.

Many tribes' and nations' stories say we came from the sky (or the stars). When asked exactly *where*, elders of many "star nations" point to the Pleiades constellation, which non-Natives call "the seven sisters," and say, "We came from there." The constellation appears to us as a tiny cloud of light, but apparently the ancients knew better. The Lakota "star blanket"—usually a quilt with one large star in the center—links us to the people of the Pleiades. Some elders of other nations say we come from water, or from the earth, or from fire.

"The Making of the World" is a sky story. This same teaching is found in the Caribbean, where this song is sung among the Cimarron: "We come from the sky, we come from the sky, go back to the sky, turn the world around!" The word *sky* is replaced by *water, fire,* and *mountain* in turn. That is the basic message of many Creation stories—go back to the roots of humanity and travel in spirit to the sky realms, to the mountain, to the water, to the fire.

4 In most Creation stories, animals recognize the importance of humans fairly quickly and try to help them survive.

☐ The Making of the World (Huron)

In the beginning was nothing but the sea, which was peopled by various creatures of the kind that live in and on the water.[1] It so happened that a woman fell down from the upper world, pushed by her husband down through a hole in the sky.[2] She was a divine personage, the sky goddess called *Ataensic* (*At-a-en-sic*) in Huron. She happened to be pregnant.[3] Two loons, which were flying over the water, happened to look up and see her falling. To save her from drowning they placed themselves beneath her, joining their bodies together to form a cushion for her to rest on. As they held her aloft, they called with a loud voice to summon the other animals to come to their aid.[4] The cry of the loon can be heard a great distance, and the other creatures of the sea heard it, and gathered together to learn

(continued on page 15)

5 The word *terrapin* derives from the Algonkian word *torope*, a variant on the Munsee *tulpe* for "turtle." Turtle is sacred because he is the foundation of all; he is Turtle Island.

6 In a similar Seneca story, the waters are filled with monsters, and so the woman must be provided with dry land. Curiously, the monsters claim they were intending to protect the woman. In the Seneca story, she eventually gives birth to six pairs of humans, male and female, representing the birth of the six nations. The Taíno of the Caribbean trace their royal family lines from a mythical female ancestress. In the Taíno tradition, it is the male god *Deminan* who mates with a female turtle, who was the ancestral mother. Most Australian Aborigines claim descent from an ancestral mother as well, in contrast to the Algonquin First *Man* (*Glooskap*, mentioned elsewhere, is one name for "First Man").

7 By working the earth, Sky Woman is a "tool of the Creator." Women did most of the planting and harvesting in Huron and Seneca societies.

8 The struggle in the womb is similar to that of the twins Jacob and Esau in Genesis 25, in which the Lord says to Rebekah, "Two nations are in your womb, two peoples quarreling while still within you ..." Esau grew to be a hunter, while Jacob became a herdsman. Jacob, the crafty one, later tricked his father on his deathbed by pretending to be Esau to gain his blessing. But Esau, the foolish one, gave up his birthright for a mess of pottage (stew).

There are tales of good and evil twins from around the world, and good and evil brothers and sisters as well. However, the use of the term *evil* may often be a later insertion, influenced by the West. The Mohawk and Mi'kmaq both object to this interpretation. In many cultures, such as the Taíno, twins are considered supernatural. We can guess that Ahura Mazda and Aharman, light and darkness respectively, in the Pahlavi texts of the Persians, are probably brothers. In Dogon lore, Yasigi, who is depicted as a large-breasted female who presides over the Sigi ceremony, has an evil twin brother Yurugu, but is protected from him by the Nommo twins. In Egyptian lore, the God Osiris

what the loons wanted. Terrapin (or snapping turtle)[5] appeared and he consented to relieve the loons of their passenger. They placed the woman on the back of the turtle, asking him to take care of her. Terrapin then called the other animals to a grand council to determine what should be done to save the life of the woman. They decided that she must have earth to live on.[6] Terrapin directed them all to dive to the bottom of the sea and bring up some earth. Many attempted it, Beaver, Muskrat, Duck, and others, but without success. Some remained below for such a long time that when they rose, they were dead. Terrapin searched their mouths but could find no clumps of earth. At last the toad went down, and after a long time, arose again, exhausted and nearly dead. On searching his mouth, Terrapin found some earth, which he gave to the woman. She took it and carefully placed it around the edge of Terrapin's shell. It grew on every side, forming at last a great land, fit for vegetation. All of this was sustained by the great Terrapin, which still supports Turtle Island today.[7]

After she landed, the woman gave birth to a daughter. Soon the daughter was made pregnant by the spirit of the terrapin, and it soon became clear she was carrying twins. While in labor, the mother heard them fighting and struggling within her womb.[8] When the time came to be born, one declared that he was willing to be born in the usual manner, like future mortals, which was to head in a downward direction. However his brother adamantly refused, saying he knew a shortcut that would save a lot of time and trouble. The one brother said, "Oh, no! We would kill our mother if we did that!" The second brother said, "If you want to go *that* way, you go first." The one brother was born, headfirst through the birth canal and received by his grandmother. The other brother had a head of flintstone (also

(continued on page 17)

is betrayed and killed by his brother Seth, who tricks him into lying down in a special sarcophagus and then seals the lid. Osiris had no evil in him, and so did not recognize a lie when he heard it. The sarcophagus floated downriver and was discovered by a king. Later Osiris was cut into fourteen pieces (some say sixteen as their are sixteen sections of the body in Egyptian lore).

9 This is clearly a teaching as to how we should take care of Mother Earth, and not destroy her. The first lesson is to not take shortcuts, but to go through life as nature intended. To show how our destinies are interlinked, Muhammad told a story about an impatient thirsty passenger on the lower deck of a ship who began to chop a hole in the hull with an ax, to obtain water more quickly. Muhammad said, "Now if they were to hold back his hand, both he and they would be saved. But if they were to leave him alone, both he and they would be doomed." Like Native American stories, the Qur'an and the Hadiths teach respect for the environment. The Hadiths are quotations from Muhammad that have been passed down since his lifetime on earth. Each one has been ranked by Islamic scholars as to the likelihood of accuracy and authenticity.

10 There is a similar story among the Cherokee, who are close cousins to the Iroquois (more correctly, Haudenosaunee, "People of the Long House"). In one version, Grandmother finds her daughter's dead body and she says, "Who did this? Who killed my daughter?" The evil boy smiles and points to the good brother and says, "*He* did it! I *saw* him!" When telling this story, it is said, "No one had ever heard a lie before, so Grandmother did not know what one was." From the beginning of time, speaking the truth has been considered a key to our mutual survival, to a good relationship with God, and for many, a way of accumulating personal power and a good reputation.

11 The good brother was also called *Yoskeha*, meaning "good man," or O*terongtongia*, which in Huron means "Maple Sprout," implying that he is a god of vegetation, but only of the sweet varieties, such as the sugar maple, most beloved of trees. It is because Tawiskarong was

called "firestone," hence his nickname, "the firestone twin"), and using it as a flint knife, he broke through his mother's side, and killed her.[9]

The grandmother was furious and said, "You have killed your mother!" But the firestone twin accused the other and argued so effectively that the grandmother threw the innocent child away into the bushes. No one had ever heard a lie before, and so she couldn't imagine the twin would say something that wasn't true.[10] The flint-like one was raised lovingly by his grandmother, while the innocent one, called the Maple Sprout, had to grow up with constant difficulties as an outcast and in constant battle with his favored, but less trustworthy brother.

The daughter was buried, and from her body sprang the sun, moon, and stars, and the various vegetables that men eat today, including, according to some, tobacco. From her head grew the pumpkin vine and its pumpkins, from her breasts grew maize; from her limbs grew beans and other vegetables.

All the while, the twins were growing up without a mother and were opposed in everything they did. The firstborn brother was called *Tijuskeha*, which some say means "good man." The second-born brother was named *Tawiskarong*, meaning "flint-like," an allusion to his hard heart and cruel nature.[11] They were not men, but supernatural beings who were to prepare the world to be a dwelling place for men. Finding they could not live together, they separated, each taking over a portion of the earth.

(continued on page 19)

made of flint that he was able to cut through the side of the mother. Likewise, certain people are "born warriors," but they do damage to their own mothers before coming of age, and thus destroy themselves. He is hard-headed, to his own detriment. One of the main tenets of Native American spirituality is that we are here to learn to be human beings, and part of being human is being vulnerable. It is said in Ojibway that a baby is born wearing no armor. This shows us that we are born with peace in our hearts, and that this is one of the greatest gifts of the Creator. Tawiskarong shows us what would happen if we were born *with* armor. Not all two-legged people have yet found what it means to truly be human, but we can't simply tell them that. In the story the two brothers are not, in fact, human beings at all, so we can point to them and criticize or idealize them, and no person will take offense. For this reason, those who are lost can perhaps see more clearly that what the hard-headed brother, Tawiskarong, does is not right. It is to be taken on faith that the good brother Tijuskeha (corresponding to *Teharonhiawako* in Mohawk) attempted every means available to him to try to make peace with his destructive brother, Tawiskarong (corresponding to *Sawiskerz* in Mohawk), before accepting the invitation to battle.

12 The giant bullfrog who steals the water shows up in many nations, but most famously with the Mi'kmaq, who call him *Agulabemu,* which means "he is without truth," or "not the right way." He too fails to take care of Mother Earth. Tijuskeha, on the other hand, does it the right way. As the Navajo say, "When you put a thing in order, give it a name, and you are all in accord, *it becomes.*"

Their first act was to create animals of various sizes and shapes and species. The flint-like brother made all the fierce and monstrous creatures: serpents, panthers, alligators, bears, giant wolves, and, of course, giant mosquitoes as large as turkeys. He tried to make human beings, but they were crippled, demonic creatures who were unable to walk. Among other things, he made an immense toad that drank up all the fresh water that was on the earth. In the meantime, Maple-Sprout, or Tijuskeha, created only innocent and useful animals.[12] They say the good brother created rivers that flowed both ways so that human beings would never have to paddle their canoes, but that the other brother created waterfalls to create barriers to people, and made rivers that flow only downstream. They say the good brother created wonderful plants for healing, and that the other brother created poisonous plants that looked just like them. They say the good brother invented flowers to fill the hands of the people and delight them, and then the other brother invented thorns.

Then the good brother made the partridge. To his surprise, the bird rose and flew toward the territory of Tawiskarong, which was off limits. Tijuskeha asked him where he thought he was going. He said he was going to look for water as there was none left in their land. He had heard there was some in the realm of Tawiskarong. Tijuskeha began to suspect some kind of mischief. He followed the course of the partridge and followed it to the land of his brother. Here he encountered snakes, serpents, and enormous biting insects, all of which he had to do battle with. Finally he came to a monstrous toad filled with water, which he cut open, letting the water flow forth in a great torrent.

The spirit of his mother warned him in a dream to beware of his brother Tawiskarong, who would try to destroy him by some trickery. Finally, the two brothers met again. It was clear by this time

(continued on page 21)

13 There is every reason to believe that Tijuskeha said this so that even if he did not survive the battle, at least one outcome would be that the seeds of corn, beans, and squash, the "three sisters" (called *deo-hako*, "the life supporters," in Seneca), which would fly in all directions as he was beaten, would be spread all over the earth—by the hand of his enemy, no less. The parallels to the "dying grain god" in world mythology are endless and deep with meaning. His death is a reference to winter.

In one version of the Mohawk story, the brothers decide to play the Native American game known to non-Natives as lacrosse, which serves as an alternative to war.

14 In the Mohawk story, the right-handed brother did not use the deer horn as a weapon, but only as a shield to deflect the spear of his brother. It is considered a symbol of peace.

15 Different Native American peoples at different times have envisioned the journey homeward to the spirit world in a different direction. Some eastern Algonquin peoples see death as an eastward journey. Some Lakota, Mayan, and Lenape (and several other tribes) say that the spirit of the deceased travels to the southwest along the spirit path that we call the Milky Way, and the stars are their footprints. In the medicine lodges of the Great Lakes, the journey of death is seen as a westward journey into the setting sun. In Celtic lore, to say that someone "went west" means that he or she died. The American western folksong "Old Paint" (collected by Carl Sandberg and Margaret Larkin) contains a possible reference to a Native American funeral custom, as the singer requests, "Oh when I die, take my saddle from the wall / put it on my pony, lead him out of his stall / tie my bones to his back, turn our faces to the west / and we'll ride the prairies that we love the best." The Algonquins are known for bone or bundle burials and, in many cases, for the idea of traveling to the west in spirit. This is also reminiscent of the Vikings (who had contact with both the Irish and the eastern Algonquins), who sent the corpse of the deceased to sea in a favorite boat and then burned the boat as it sailed into the sunset, a westward direction.

that they could not both live together on the earth, that the planet wasn't big enough for the both of them. They decided that they should engage in formal combat to decide which of them would remain master of the world.

Because they were supernatural beings, they then realized that the battle might last forever, so each decided to let the other know what weapon he could not overcome. The good brother stated that he could be destroyed only by being beaten to death with a bag full of corn, beans, and squash, or some manner of breads. The evil brother answered by saying he could only be killed by the horn of a deer, or other wild horned animal. They made a map of the area in which the fighting should take place.

Tawiskarong had the first turn. He set upon his brother with a bag of corn, beans, and squash, chased him around the field of battle until he was nearly lifeless and lay as if dead.[13] He revived, through the aid of his mother's spirit, and, recovering his strength, pursued his evil brother, beating him with a deer's horn until he killed him.[14]

But Tawiskarong was not totally destroyed. He reappeared to his brother in a vision, and told him that he was going away to the west, and that henceforth all Native people after death would go to the west to dwell in spirit form.[15]

2
The Wager for the World

▤ This story follows the thread of the Huron Creation story from chapter 1. As before, the use of the word "evil" is questionable.

☐1 Malsum is actually a wolf, although this may be of Viking origin, as there is no negative association with the wolf in Mi'kmaq culture. There is a story of an evil wolf in the Eddas (Ragnarok) called Moongarm, who is of the night, and who devours the moon during the course of an eclipse. He is filled with the lifeblood of all dead men and stains the heavens with blood. The Eddas are two ancient literary collections of Icelandic sagas, or stories, the prose Edda and the poetic Edda.

☐2 It is highly probable that there was a version of the Mohawk Creation story in which two brothers try to decide the fate of the world through a peach stone gambling game as an alternative to war. In the Mi'kmaq version of the game, called *woltestakun,* the player slaps the platter on the leather or cloth square on the ground in a way that makes the peach pits pop up in the air and fly around like birds.

Why is this game considered to be so spiritual? Within the Native tradition it is thought that reality proceeds from the inner world to the outer, and vice versa, so that our beliefs and expectations can affect certain aspects of reality and that reality affects certain aspects of our beliefs. Some say that the Creator alone decides who wins and loses the peach pit game, but others say they are "testing their medicine" when they play.

☐3 Gambling played a major role in the formative periods of many world religions, and it is a large part of Native American spirituality as well. Kathryn Gabriel, who has researched this extensively, writes, "Although it may seem to be a contradiction in terms, gambling is as spiritual as praying. Both activities seek divine affirmation and reversal of fortune." The Ojibway/Chippewa game "bowl and counters" (*pugasaing*), is described in a gambling sequence in Henry Wadsworth Longfellow's *The Song of Hiawatha.*

In Isaiah 34:17, dice were cast in order to determine land allotments given to each family to pass on from one generation to the next. Urim

☐ The Chickadee Story (Mi'kmaq)

In many ancient stories around the world there are twin brothers at the beginning of the human race, a good brother and an evil brother. So it is with this story. The two brothers both want control of the earth, but one wants to make life better for the future race of mankind, one wants to make it worse. The world is new and full of life, yet already it isn't big enough for the both of them. They are miserable and constantly at war. The evil brother, *Malsum*,[1] wishes to continue fighting as long as necessary in order to decide who will prevail over the earth, but the good brother, *Glooskap*, suggests that instead of this endless war, they compete in a peach pit game, a gambling game called *woltis* (or *woltestakun* [**wol**-*test*-**a**-*kun*]),[2] winner take all. The evil brother agrees, and goes first.

The evil brother takes the six peach pits, black on one side, white on the other, and places them in the peach pit platter, a long, flat bowl designed to catch peach pit halves. He flips the bowl upward, the peach pits roll and tumble in the air, and they fall back down, all black, the white sides facing down, a perfect score.

The evil brother laughs an evil laugh, and then hands the bowl and peach pits to his brother, who can only tie by making a perfect score, either all six white or all six black.

The good brother holds the platter, but prays to the Creator. He says, "Creator, if you have any mercy on the earth and the human beings to come, please show your power and help me with this peach pit throw."[3]

(continued on page 27)

and Thummim were the names of two divining stones employed by priests as instruments for discovering God's will. These stories were also used by Saul and David, and are also mentioned in Ezra and Nehemiah. In Exodus 28:30, God tells Moses that whenever Aaron comes into his presence in holy places, he must carry the Urim and Thummim in his breastpiece engraved with the names of the tribes of Israel so that he could "bear the judgment of the people of Israel upon his heart before the Lord continually." In so doing, God would always remember his people, and Aaron could determine his will for Israel. Thummim means "perfect things" and was probably the *yes* symbol, leaving Urim to be the *no* symbol. Each of the two stones would have carried both symbols, one on each side. Presumably, two *no* sides meant no, two *yes* sides meant yes, and one of each indicated no answer.

Life is often a gamble, and may we have to make important, bold decisions based on insufficient information. As the saying goes, "He who hesitates is lost," hence the spirit of risk-taking can be an asset in a spirit-led life. At times like those, we must trust Spirit to guide our steps in the right direction, even if it feels as if we are jumping off a cliff. When Moses and Aaron made decisions based on a throwing of the Thummim and Urim, we assume they were doing a lot of praying at the same time, just like Glooskap. The Native American divination practice of throwing the cowry shells is yet more similar and may in fact be the origin of the peach pit game. Cowry shells and peach pits are similarly shaped.

4 The black-capped chickadee (which says its name, *chickadeedeedee*) can be seen as a bird of peace because it is created from the miracle of the peach pit game. The bird is shaped like a large, whole peach pit, black on the top half and white on the bottom half, but five inches in length.

He prays again to Creator and flips the peach pits up into the sky.
The pits spin in the air, black-white-black-white-black-white, and
stay suspended as if held up by some miraculous power. The evil
brother stands horrified, cursing louder and louder, while the good
brother stands amazed, trying to prepare to catch the whirling disks.
Gradually, the peach pits turn into gentle chickadees, those tiny
black and white birds. The birds fly away, and so the game could
never be resolved. That is why there are chickadees, why there is still
gambling, and why there are still evil people around, not to mention
good ones.[4]

1 Most, if not all, cultures recognized and personified the elements of the sky as spirit beings or gods, if only as devices to tell teaching stories. Thunder, lightning, sun, moon, wind, and so forth, were all very dramatic visual aids for storytellers. Thunder, sun, moon, fire, wind, and water were known to the highly civilized Greeks as Zeus, Apollo, Artemis, Haephestus, Zephyr, and Poseidon. Until recently, it was seen as a mark of distinction among the educated to know these nature spirits by name. But how many can utter the Natchez names for these spirits off the top of their heads?

2 The Wise Old Man is another name for Creator, sometimes referred to as Coyote Old Man and various other names. He is a strange character, and in one story he steals the sun's leggings. In some stories he is a little bit of a trickster. Here, he is explicitly appearing as his Father Sky aspect: fatherly, wise, and gentle. Some say he lives at the end of the journey through the spirit world. There he sits by a warm fire, rocking in his rocking chair (or sitting on a stump, or the like), and he is willing to talk to those who know how to find him. But if you walk past him and go through the tent flap behind him, you will never return to your body on earth and you will die. Coyote Old Man was here before humankind and makes the stars and moon, the rainbows, and the sun in the sky, and he shares them with humans without really seeming to be concerned with it all.

☐ The Adoption of the Human Race (Natchez)

In the very beginning, Moon, Sun, Wind, Rainbow, Thunder, Fire, and Water[1] once met a very old man. This wise old man turned out to be Chief of the Sky Spirits.[2] Thunder asked him, "Can you make the people of the world my children?"

"No, no, no!" Wise Old Man replied. "They cannot be your children but they can be your grandchildren."

Sun asked Old Man, "Can you make the people of the world my children?"

"No, they cannot be your children," answered Old Man. "But they can be your friends and grandchildren. Your main purpose is to give plenty of light."

Moon asked, "Can you make the people of the world my children?"

"No, no, I cannot do that," Old Man replied. "The people of the world can be your nephews and friends."

Fire asked that the people of the world be made his children.

Wise Old Man replied, "No, I cannot give them to you to be your children, but the people of the world can be your grandchildren. You can be their warmth and give them fire to cook their food."

(continued on page 31)

29

3 | In this story, Old Man's teaching is for parents. All of us as adults have a special area that we excel in, whether it is making fire, making friends, healing people, cooking, providing warmth and shelter, or shedding light on ancient mysteries. The sun, moon, fire, rainbow, and rainwater all represent our different talents as adults. As we raise our children, we have a tendency to want to create them in our own image, because after all they are *our* children. We think they belong to us, and that we have the right to control them. In fact, sometimes we think we are their Creator and start to step into Old Man's shoes.

We can see that those who try to force their children to live a certain way are often disappointed. Their efforts are met with rebellion and scorn, or complete indifference and ingratitude.

In Native American culture, with some tribal groups more than others, we are to let children find their own path in life, to become as Creator intended them to be. Children learn to make their own decisions wisely if they get practice, early and often. As people of every culture have noticed, grandparents have the best time with children. Because they don't have parental responsibilities, they can just play and try to discover who that child really is—a rainbow, a star, a thundercloud—and then let them blossom according to their nature.

This story tells us that is not such a bad way to raise a child, because they are not our children anyway. We are all children of Father Sky and Mother Earth (a few tribes say Father Earth and Mother Sky, or Grandfather Sun and Grandmother Moon, which is fine for our purposes); we are the holy infant that completes the sacred trinity when we are in a sacred space. We are supposed to maintain an innocent, childlike attitude of trust toward our divine "parents" even when we have children of our own. This path in Algonkian tongues is called *tchichankweewee* (**tchi**-chan-**kwee**-wee), which means "Great Spirit watch over me." This is the path of the heart in Algonquin traditions, very much in the spirit of the devotional or Bhakti path of yoga of India, and all other devotional paths from around the world.

Wind asked the same question as the others. Wise Old Man told Wind, "No, no, the people of the world cannot be your children, but they can be your grandchildren. You can remove the bad air and all kinds of diseases from the people, and keep them healthy."

Rainbow wanted the people to be his children. "No, they cannot be your children," Wise Old Man explained. "You will always be busy preventing too much rain and floods upon the earth."

Water asked that human beings be made his children, but Wise Old Man answered, "No, the people of the world can never be your children. When they get dirty, you must always be available to wash them clean. You shall give them long life."

Wise Old Man continued, "I have now told all of you the best ways to guide yourselves and what you can do to help the people of the world. You must always remember that these children of the human race are *my children!*"[3]

▤ There have long been Native American teachings about the destructive power of gambling, which are preserved in the famous Co-No stories of the Winnebago. I have combined and updated these stories in order to make a comment on some of the excesses that have been heaped upon what was once a form of divination—gambling. *Cono* in Hotcąk (Winnebago language) means "to do wrong," or "to sin." That should have been a red flag to the humans in this story, and to people today who may have gambling addiction disorders and do not seek help.

1 I place the Winnebago first because the Co-No stories are of Winnebago origin, and they are the ones who named him Co-No, as a warning to others.

2 Gambling has been a popular pastime with Native Americans for centuries, and so it is likely that certain people developed what we would call gambling addictions, even back then.

3 The "three sisters"—corn, beans, and squash—are considered sacred gifts from Creator. Clearly, the people are addicted and doing wrong at this point. They are trapped in the evil one's game. It gets worse.

☐ Co-No, the World's Greatest Gambler (Winnebago)

One day many aeons ago, a tall, handsome, and well-dressed brave, calling himself "Co-No, the World's Greatest Gambler," came to Turtle Island to offer his expertise to the Native American nations, at least the ones with strong gambling traditions. He told them that as their gambling consultant he would charge them no fee, but would simply like to show them the real meaning of gambling. This he would do by giving them free gaming lessons.

"What's the catch?" they all asked. He answered that in order to make the teachings more effective, they had to wager against him in real games, with real stakes.

"What games did you have in mind?" they asked.

"Any game you can play!" he answered, brimming with confidence.

The Winnebago agreed,[1] and then all the other tribes agreed as well. Unbeknownst to them, Co-No was not a human being but a powerful spirit bent on misusing his magical powers to win from them all their wampum and possessions. He won every game and yet the human beings would not stop playing him.[2]

After their gambling bags were empty, they cried out, "How can we keep playing? We have no more to wager!" Co-No said he would be willing to play them for their right to grow plants such as corn, beans, and squash, as well as their right to hunt, to give them a chance to win back what they had lost.[3] He would even throw in

(continued on page 35)

4 | In one version, the storyteller says they lost their rights to "the things of the earth." I have paraphrased it slightly to bring the message more up to date.

5 | In most Native societies, the first and foremost priority of men is to protect the women and children, who are smaller and less muscular, and who represent the future existence of the tribe. Again, we are supposed to be outraged at this injustice. The listener is supposed to jump up and exclaim, "No! Not the women and children too!" And yet gambling addiction takes its toll on the families of gamblers every day.

6 | Rabbit is described as the "son of the Great Spirit" in Winnebago. In Eastern Algonkian, he is called *Waboose,* a most powerful spirit. I believe *Wakjonkaga* (**Wak**-jon-**ka**-ga)—described as another son of the Great Spirit—means Raven Man in Winnebago (Hotcâk).

7 | Saying he was "not as he should be" means he was not on the Red Road, and was not "following his original instructions." This means that gambling of this type is not part of the Red Road. In certain source material, Co-No was cast aside and sent to the north, as imperfect and unfinished. The same source material describes Co-No as the source of all evil, even though he was "created by the Great Spirit."

their right to use the tree medicines and the fruits and nuts, as part of their stakes.

The trusting humans, who were not too bright in those days, agreed to all he suggested. One by one, they lost the use of the beans, grains, and gourds, the fruits, the berries, and then the hooved and pawed animals, and the little mammals, and finally the fish as well. They lost their beautiful environment which had been preserved carefully for a hundred previous generations.[4]

Again the people cried out, "We are completely spent! We have no more to wager," but Co-No stroked his chin and answered, "I see you are in quite a bind. You have nothing to eat, no clothing, shelter, firewood, so you must keep playing day and night to win back what you have lost. We must think of some more stakes. Something truly valuable. What about all your women and children?"

Seeing no other way out, the men put forth their utmost efforts, and gambled with the demon, but within four days, they had lost all the women and children as well. It was a sad day.[5]

Co-No consolidated all his winnings into huge piles. He placed all the corn in one small field near his lodge, to guard it. He took all the maples and, using his magic, made them into one large maple tree that flowed with thick syrup. Then he took all the women and, using his magic, made from them one beautiful woman to be his wife, and all the children became one child. These things he guarded jealously. Meanwhile, men began to suffer and starve.

Soon the spirits of Rabbit, Turtle, Thunder, and a great being called *Wakjonkaga*[6] came among the people in the shape of human beings, and told them that Co-No was no gambling consultant but an evil spirit who was created before humankind was upon the earth. Rabbit recounted how Co-No was then cast aside by the Creator because he was imperfect, "not as he should be."[7] Rabbit said that this being was filled with jealousy and anger against the human race

(*continued on page 37*)

This seems like a later addition, perhaps influenced by the story of the angel Samael (*sam* means poison, and *el* means angel, according to the Second Book of Enoch and Rabbinical literature such as the Zohar), who was cast out of heaven, and came to be "the source of all evil," Lucifer.

8 Some elders insist that all animals are good, but certain animals and birds have negative connotations within certain tribes. Bat is disliked by the Algonquins, but revered by the Taíno. Owl is liked by some tribes and feared by others. The storyteller decides which animals are allies of Co-No.

9 Jackstraws is a game where the player drops a handful of thin sticks and then forces a pointed stick down through the middle of the pile to divide out an odd or even number.

10 Partridge is considered a glory-seeker whose vanity is not appreciated by some Native Americans. We wonder if Co-No appealed to Partridge's pride to get him to join him. Partridge was the one who left Tijuskeha to investigate the dark side of the world in "The Making of the World." Tijuskeha followed Partridge into his brother's hellish realm. Crane, on the other hand, is a power animal who signifies patience and is the peacemaker among birds.

11 Stare is a game where two players sit and stare at each other with wide-open eyes. The first one to blink loses.

12 Owl is considered a messenger of death, and a night bird of prey, and so some tribal groups fear Owl and associate him with evil. Others say he is the messenger from the unconscious and the spirit world in general, and is good.

and was to be avoided at all costs. Then Rabbit and his friends found Co-No in his posh wigwam and challenged him to a game.

Co-No asked what they had to play for. They answered coyly that they would put up their bodies as stakes, as there was nothing much to live for. Co-No was delighted. On the day of the games, Rabbit and his allies stood on one side, and Co-No and all his bad spirits stood on the other.[8] Co-No suggested they play Jackstraws.[9] When all the sticks were dropped, Co-No was the first to play. He brought Partridge to do the playing for him.[10] Instead of using a pointed stick, Partridge forced his bill down the center of the pile and separated out an even number. But Turtle took such a long, deep breath that he inhaled one of the sticks, making an odd number and causing Partridge and Co-No to lose.

It was Rabbit's turn, and he brought with him a tall, blue crane with a very long bill, to divide the sticks for him. Crane stepped up and forced his long bill down through the center of the sticks, dividing out an even dozen. The animals had won an important victory for the people, and so they went home carrying many of their former possessions.

Naturally, Co-No was eager to play another game, so another day was set. On that day, Co-No wanted to play a game of Stare.[11] Rabbit and his allies had a meeting, and were sure that Co-No would bring along his buddy Owl to do his staring for him.[12] No other animal or bird had a chance against Owl in a staring contest, so Rabbit decided that Wakjonkaga should try. Thunder took Wakjonkaga aside and they whispered together, then Wakjonkaga came out and sat facing Owl. For the better part of the morning, they sat staring at each other without closing their eyes, or winking the least bit. Wakjonkaga started to squirm in his seat. Thunder flew over their heads and shot a raindrop into Owl's eye with a great clap

(continued on page 39)

13 This passage reminds me of the Cuban Missile Crisis, Khrushchev's great gamble for the world, which made an impression on me as a youth growing up in Washington, D.C. My father said that we were "eyeball to eyeball with the Russians, and the other fellow just blinked." This story pre-dates that remark (originally made by Secretary of State Dean Rusk) by hundreds of years, and predicts much of what is happening today as well.

14 The game of Pegs uses a four-sided peg numbered on each side, and with pointed ends, so that when it is struck with a stick, it will fly up. The number that is visible when it lands is the number of points won by the player who strikes it.

15 Forked Man was a popular fantasy character with two complete bodies above the waist and one set of legs below, like a forked stick. In fact, such mutations do occasionally occur in mammals, so it is possible they happen to humans.

16 As you see, this is yet another story where humans make mistakes, this time by associating with the wrong kind of spirit beings, and have to be rescued by animals who know better. As the Cree say, "Animals don't make mistakes, people do." Perhaps they know that the earth does not belong to them, but that they belong to the earth.

of thunder. Owl blinked. The human beings sent up a great shout of joy. They had won the day. Again, the people went home bearing more of their belongings.[13]

It was decided that on the third day, they would play Pegs.[14] Rabbit and his allies suggested the location should be at a certain lodge, the lodge of Forked Man.[15] Co-No agreed and brought the remaining stakes to the lodge. They played for hours without a clear winner. By prior arrangement, Forked Man came home, acted surprised, and, brandishing a huge club, asked, "Who gave you permission to gamble in my lodge?" and ordered them out. In all the confusion and excitement, Rabbit and his friends grabbed the stakes and ran away. And that is how the animals won the human beings back their freedom.[16]

3
The Origins
of Fire

1 The opening words of this story are the same words that open many of the fire stories. If Native stories are an unwritten Bible, an "oral Torah," this is Genesis, verse 1, chapter 1. As the invention of writing is a marker and symbol to the Western world of the birth of civilization, fire is a symbol of civilization to the Native American. It permeates all aspects of culture and has countless meanings, including God, life, a unit of government such as a sachemdom, illumination, vision, the ancestors, power, different aspects of male and female power, and on and on. The Hindus too have preserved the spiritual creation of fire in sacred story. In fact, the oldest of the Vedas describes a society where man had no fire, no protection against wild beasts, and uncertainty of prey. It too encapsulates the development of this important force on earth as a parallel to spiritual awakening, as does this Cherokee story.

Like the Greek myths of Prometheus, those who first dared to bring fire to humankind or animalkind were harmed in some way, because they were not familiar with its properties and didn't know how to handle it. It was a long learning process in which many died. And yet once fire was easily available, it made life a great deal better for everyone. It is one of the first things Native people thank Creator for in their prayers. The Cherokee say, "Each morning upon rising and each morning before sleeping, give thanks for the life within you and for all life, for good things Creator has given you, and for the opportunity to grow a little more each day."

2 Sycamore trees date back to a time before the ice age. In southern regions, this would be particularly true. In fact, sycamores are some of the oldest-living trees in North America, and often live to be over eight hundred years old. These trees can be several yards across. The old ones also tend to become hollow and are therefore more susceptible to catching fire. Some early Native Americans used ground hollows in trees for shelter, and the sycamore hollows were so large, they were as big as a small wigwam. It is known that early European settlers would use them as fireplaces as well, but it shortens the life of the tree.

☐ The First Fire (Cherokee)

In the beginning there was no fire.[1]

The world was very cold. One day, a long time ago, the Thunders who lived in the sky sent their lightning and put fire into the bottom of a hollow sycamore tree that grew on an island.[2] The animals knew the fire was there because they could see the

(continued on page 45)

The Algonquin Nation elders of the Ottawa Valley say that in 1833, the great tree by the council fire on Victoria Island in the Ottawa River, right next to the Parliament Building, was hit by lightning and was turned black and continued to smoke for an entire year. It may have been a sycamore. Perhaps large trees on islands are more vulnerable to catching fire because those at the edge of the water would be exposed to the open sky. In any case, sycamores were sacred because the ancestors used them for shelter, and they enjoyed a status similar to ancestral caves. Note that the story specifies that it was a sycamore tree, not any other. This denotes that the story happened a long time ago.

3 There is an important tradition of holding council fire meetings on islands in rivers throughout North America. This dates back at least two thousand, if not three thousand, years. These islands are often near waterfalls, and are connected by Native American trails, transcontinental roadways that stretch from sea to sea. There are many reasons for this tradition, one of which is practical: an island is easier to defend than any other spot and is easy to reach by boat. And as hoofed animals cross rivers at island crossings, there was already a trail going to it! These islands may have been the birthplaces of Native American culture as we know it; in fact, it seems that they were revered by Native people hundreds of years before European contact as a place of pilgrimage to be with the ancestors.

4 In one Iroquois version of the story, the birds fly to the sun to try to capture its fire. In the Cherokee version, we assume the tree was hit by lightning before the story begins, but the animals don't know that. The tree becomes a burning bush of sorts, a symbol of the Creator's mystical power.

5 Vulture (*Suli* in Cherokee), is very proud of his plumage, which of course we never get to see, as all vultures today are bald—and presumably very humble.

6 This bird does not appear in the version recorded by the well-known anthropologist Mooney, but it appears in others, and it highlights the

smoke coming out at the top of the tree, and they wanted to warm themselves. But they could not get to it because of the water. So they held a council to decide what to do.[3]

Every animal that could fly or swim was eager to go get the fire.[4] Vulture, or *Suli* in Cherokee, was the largest of the birds, and was greatly admired for the wonderful plume he had on his head.[5] When the moment arrived, everyone turned to him with expectant faces. He flew up to the tree and captured an ember of the flame. With nowhere else to put it, he placed it on his head and wrapped it in his beautiful plumage. On the way back, he smelled something burning. The smell got stronger and stronger. Suddenly he felt a burning sensation on his head, and he screamed out, "*Ahhhgh!* I've been burned." He shook his head and the ember fell in the water and turned to smoke with a great fizzling sound. When he arrived back on dry land, everyone was staring at him with shock. He felt the top of his head. His beautiful plumage, the pride of his clan, was gone. He was bald![6]

(continued on page 47)

"humble yourself" message, which is the message of all ordeals and fasting. This is clearer in the Iroquois version than in the Cherokee. The vulture is not viewed as bad but is thought of as a helpful bird, the long-suffering "garbage man" of the avian kingdom. In fact, Vulture plays an important role in the Creation story. He fanned the wet, muddy earth with his wings, and the upsweep of his curved wingtips created the mountain ranges of the Smokies.

7 *Anitsisqua (A-ni-tsis-qua)* is the Cherokee Bird Clan, and they have a special role in society as messengers, as well as protectors of the winged people. Raven is also a messenger, and warns of danger. The raven is associated with fire and the sun (the god Lugh) in Celtic lore. The raven, the blackest of birds, black as burnt wood (who was originally pure white, according to the Cherokee), has been burned by fire, and yet there is no concept of fire as evil, and no association whatsoever with "fires of hell." In high-tech society, we are taught that all fire is bad. In Native society, all fire is good. It is said in Indian country that a white fire man puts out a fire, whereas a red fire man starts a fire. A fire man or fire keeper is a very important role, similar in some ways to a priest or minister, parallel to the highly esteemed *Agni-hotras* of India who preside over powerful fire rituals with great skill. In a number of lodges in Canada today, only those of certain family lineages are allowed to be fire keepers, and yet, like the fireman of the modern world, this job does *not* tend to attract the lazy, the glory-seeking, or the vain. Even the most skilled Native fire keepers face injury every time they go near the fire. It is not unusual even for experienced fire keepers to have their eyebrows singed off from the heat of a large fire, or strands of their long hair, or a mustache, especially when working with a "Y stick" (a stick cut from the fork in a tree) as a ceremonial tool.

8 In the Iroquois fire stories, the message of "humble yourself before the power of Creator" is clear. Here it is more subtle. Contact with this uncontrolled, untamed power has a way of finding your weakness and reminding you of your mortality. Fire is a great purifier. A fire connected to a sweat lodge or teaching lodge is a sacred fire, and no garbage is to be put into it, not even a cigarette. Although cigarettes

Raven offered to go. Because he was so large and strong and smart, all the others thought he should go next. They all admired him for his beautiful feathers of many colors. He flew high and far across the water and, alighting on the sycamore tree, gazed at the flame, wondering what to do. While he was thinking and thinking, the heat scorched all his feathers black, and he became frightened and flew away. He arrived back at the gathering of disappointed animals empty-handed, and without any fire. They were shocked to see his beautiful colored feathers turned black.[7]

Sharp-eyed little Screech Owl volunteered to go. He reached the island safely, but while he was looking down into the hollow tree, a blast of hot air came up and nearly burned out his eyes. He flew home as best he could, but it was a long time before he could see well. The eyes of little Screech Owl are red to this day.[8]

(continued on page 49)

are filled with tobacco, which is sacred, *they* are not sacred because the filter tips are not traditional. No piece of paper, no wrapper, goes into the fire—only that which is made by the Creator directly, or the sacred bundles and trade cloths for healing the people, because they are blessed in the lodge.

9 As with all stories in the "Why?" genre, in this story children and adults are made more acutely aware of the features of different creatures of the forest, in this case, the birds. This gives a tongue-in-cheek credibility to these fictional stories and helps educate the young about identifying birds.

10 The snake is more humble than the colorful bird, but is still related to the serpent, and a possible source of trouble. The snake's "medicine," its inherent power and survival skill, has a dark and a light side, as with that of most creatures. In some Native American stories, snakes are good because they shed their skin and start over afresh. In Celtic lore they are associated with the goddess Brigid and with the spirit of the land. They are divinatory. In Scottish tradition, the snake emerges from the hill at Imbolc, the holiday coinciding with Brigid's feast day, Candlemas, and Groundhog Day. If the snake becomes active, it will be a short winter; if it returns quickly to its hole, it will be a long winter. Because there are no snakes in Ireland, the hedgehog plays the same role there.

On the dark side, snakes are portrayed as opportunists who get larger and larger and end up eating everything, and they "speak with a forked tongue." This image was invoked in the speech by Cherokee Chief Speckled Snake, who said sneeringly of the Great White Father Andrew Jackson in 1833, "He loves his red children, and his tongue is not forked." He was being ironic, as Jackson was already famed as an "Indian fighter" before he became president, and was at that point in the process of removing all Cherokee legal rights and moving the Cherokee westward, partly through trickery and highly rhetorical speeches. Jackson's subsequent Treaty of New Echota was lambasted for its double dealing by none other than Daniel Webster, whose tongue was said to have been made from silver.

Then Hooting Owl and Horned Owl went, as they too were proud of their good vision. But by the time they got to the hollow tree, the fire was burning so fiercely the smoke nearly blinded them, and the ashes carried up by the wind made white rings around their eyes. They had to come home without fire. And for all their rubbing, they were never able to get rid of the white rings.[9]

Now no more of the birds would dare to approach the tree. So the little colorful snake, now called Black Racer, said he would go through the water and bring back some fire. He swam across to the island and crawled through the grass to the tree and went into a small hole at the bottom. The heat and smoke were too much for him, too. After dodging about blindly over the hot ashes until he was almost on fire, he managed by good luck to get out again at the same hole. But his body had been scorched black. And he has ever since had the habit of darting and doubling back on his track, as if trying to escape from close quarters or rearing back from intense heat.

He came back, and the great blacksnake, Climber, offered to go for the fire. He swam over to the island and climbed up the tree on the outside as the blacksnake always does. But when he put his head down into the tree, the smoke choked him and he fell into the burning stump. Before he could climb out, he was as black as little Black Racer.[10]

(continued on page 51)

11 The four-leggeds are associated with the *Anitsaguhi* (**A**-nee-tsa-**gu**-hee), the Bear Clan; the *Aniwayha* (**A**-nee-**way**-ha), the Wolf Clan; or the *Aniawi* (**A**-nee-**a**-wee), the Deer Clan. This part of the story describes the "Chicken Little" effect, where there is a job to be done and no one wants to do it. Any face-to-face community must find solutions to deal with this type of attitude, which is part of the human condition. Because free will is the basis of so many Native American societies, no one is told what to do, or forced to do it, unless it is truly a matter of life or death. Teaching tales such as this instill a sense of tribal responsibility from early childhood, so that members will be glad to take the risk voluntarily.

As with other cultures around the world, the myth of the hero's journey evolves in stages. The earliest and purest form of hero is not a show-off but is chosen by circumstance, by a twist of fate, as was the young Arthur when he pulled Excalibur from a stone or when Moses was found in the rushes of the Nile. The hero then saves the day, not with violence, but with scrappy cleverness and resourcefulness. The heroes of Woodland Indian stories are generally of this nature. The permeating message is that problems are not easily solved, but that violence does not solve them. It is only through using every nonviolent means at our disposal—clever thinking, physical perseverance, kindness, and prayer—that we can resolve intertribal conflicts. For the most part, it is disrespectful to refer to such heroes as "tricksters."

It is only in more complex, highly agricultural societies that you find the war hero myth emerge, with its attention to weaponry and fidelity to the leader. The hero with a thousand faces described by Joseph Campbell in his book by the same name has a few warrior aspects, but is predominantly the tribal type of hero who stumbles into awareness of a danger that threatens his people and "brings a boon to his village" by ingenuity. Like Parsifal, the hero is pure of heart. Like King Arthur, the hero is humble when selected for heroism.

Now the animals held another council, for still there was no fire and the world was still cold. But birds, snakes, and four-footed animals all had some excuse for not going. They were all afraid to venture near the burning sycamore tree.[11] But Water Spider at last said she would go. She was not the water spider that looks like a mosquito, but the other one with black downy hair and red stripes on

(continued on page 53)

12 In the "Mud Diver Story" of Creation as told by the Munsee Delaware, there is no land yet; it is an earlier stage of Creation. There are many parallels between the two stories. Here, Water Spider is the smallest and humblest of all the creatures (plus, she is a female, an encouraging message to young women). Grandmother Spider also represents the web of life, which shows us how we are all related. If we realize what this means, we will be compassionate to each other, as Grandmother Spider is. The word *takaful* in Islamic tradition refers to cosmic symbiosis, the web of life by which God sustains all living things. Muhammad said, "The compassionate are shown compassion by the All-Compassionate. Show compassion to those on earth and He Who is in Heaven will show compassion to you." So, there is truth in this story on many levels. Most important, it is true that we never know who among us is going to find a strength beyond themselves and become the hero, and who is going to run away. As we say, "You never know who you're talking to."

13 In a tribal society, all weaknesses become self-evident, and the stronger and larger members of the tribe can intimidate the lesser. That's why it is of utmost importance that everyone feel needed and respected, even indispensable. Elders trying to help the small and weak to remain confident in "the system" can use stories like this as parables to bolster their confidence, and show that the littlest and humblest tribe members can turn out to be the most important. The spider is by far the smallest of the creatures mentioned. Children especially appreciate that part. It is said in Cherokee, "Treat every person, from the tiniest child to the eldest elder, with respect at all times."

14 Again, there is the tongue-in-cheek "proof" of the story in the features of Water Spider today, including her ability to weave from spun thread, and the existence of fire. Told around a campfire, the storyteller can dramatically point to the fire and say, "There it is! Let's all thank courageous Water Spider!"

her body. She can run on top of the water or dive to the bottom. She would have no trouble getting to the island. But how could she bring back the fire?[12]

"I'll manage that," said Water Spider Woman.[13] Whereupon she spun a thread from her body and wove it into a bowl that she fastened to her back. Then she crossed to the island and went through the grass to where the fire was still burning. She put one little coal of fire into her bowl and came back with it. Ever since, we have had fire, and Water Spider still has her bowl on her back today.[14]

1 This is the same advice given to Weesuckerjack of the Cree in "The Boy That Wanted to Fly with the Eagles," which is included in my book *No Word for Time*. Here, Fox is portrayed as a trickster, as Coyote usually is. As with most tricksters, Fox has both a sacred and profane nature. He does good in spite of himself, and also makes a fool of himself by making mistakes and using poor judgment. He is often prone to vanity and greed. We can only guess why he wants to learn the call of the geese, but it is probably to lure them to be hunted and killed.

2 If the fire refers symbolically to some form of power, then the realization of that power could indeed lead to a "fall" from grace for those too foolish to handle it. Flying on eagles' wings, or geese's wings, is a metaphor for the spiritual life of a pipe carrier, fire keeper, or holy man or woman. In order to keep going by "following the spirit," we must keep our balance every second, and not be pulled this way or that, or be pulled downward by the gravity of human desire. We must keep our medicine good. In a similar way, Weesuckerjack, in one version of the Cree story, looked down to where some Cree women were bathing, lost his balance, and fell into the river. There are many similar stories. It is one of the best illustrations of a great fundamental teaching of indigenous North America: Keep your balance!

3 Fireflies might be "keepers of a big fire," because fireflies often mass together on walls and tree trunks by the hundreds, if not thousands, and this is apparently more common in the South than in other regions of North America. Heat seems to have an effect in triggering the phenomenon. When amassed in this way, they flash on and off in exact synchronicity. The result is apparently bright, like fire, and unforgettable, hence the name *fire*flies.

The firefly village may be a historical reference, now lost, to a neighboring people, perhaps whites, whose village was stockaded, and who had great stockpiles of firewood and fire-making tools, or "strike-a-lights," which the Apache wanted to "borrow." This, of course, is speculation, but the story does evoke such an image, probably deliberately, and continues to make the fireflies sound human.

□ Fire-Stealing Fox (Jicarilla-Apache)

Long ago, animals and trees talked with each other, but there was no fire at that time.

Fox was most clever, and he tried to think of a way to bring fire to the world. One day, he decided to visit the geese, *tetl*, whose cry he wished to learn to imitate. They promised to teach him if he would fly with them. So they contrived a way to attach wings to Fox, but cautioned him never to open his eyes while flying.[1]

Whenever the geese arose in flight, Fox also flew along with them to practice their cry. On one such adventure, darkness descended suddenly as they flew over the village of the fireflies, *konatcica* (*ko-na-tseek-a*). In mid-flight, the glare from the flickering fireflies caused Fox to forget and he opened his eyes. Instantly his wings collapsed! His fall was uncontrollable.[2] He landed within the walled area of the firefly village, where a fire constantly burned in the center.[3] Two

(continued on page 57)

4 Certain juniper berries, the gray and blue, which only grow on junipers native to Texas such as the Pinchot juniper (the cedar tree family), are said to be highly poisonous, but if taken in small bites can induce visions and journeys. Some consider them a sacred ceremonial plant. Why Fox would give these in the form of a necklace to fireflies is not clear, but they may have been highly valued at that time. Since fireflies could not literally wear a necklace, we suspect these are people, and not fireflies. If the fireflies were white people, perhaps he wanted them to hallucinate so that he could more easily take fire from them.

5 It was common for clay pits to be located near springs and drinking water and common for villages to be near clay pits. Colored clay is a source of spiritual power, and is traditionally used as a healing balm applied directly to injuries, as a body paint, and as a source for ceremonial paint. It can also be used for pottery. Jicarilla (Hi-ko-**ree**-a) derives from the Spanish word for potter, *ollero*.

6 Again, there is a sacred reference here as well as a possible historic one. The white fox is the oversoul of the foxes, the Great Spirit Fox. He would be the one prayed to in order to acquire some of the attributes of the fox, such as cleverness, quick thinking, sexual ability, or independence and ability to escape. He is associated with the males, as the otter is with the females. In some tribes, the men will paint themselves white to become a *Manitoo* ("spirit" or "ghost") while dancing around a ceremonial fire.

Among most indigenous peoples throughout the world, there is both a "shadow soul" (the higher self, or soul) and a "blood soul," which is what we, in English, call a "ghost." However, the settlers who first met the Native Americans used the word "ghost" for both "shadow soul" and "blood soul," and, thus, the subtlety is lost. A similar distinction appears in biblical references to the Holy Ghost. It is really holy *spirit*, a Latin word associated with breath (*Geist* in German), and also is related to the Hebrew word *rûah*, "wind" or "breath," which is used four hundred times in the Hebrew scriptures to refer to spirit. In Native American tradition, the shadow soul is always seen as a white light or white figure, animal, or person. This was one

kindly fireflies came to see fallen Fox, who gave each one a necklace of juniper berries, *katlteitse* (*katl-tay-ee-tsay*).[4]

Fox hoped to persuade the two fireflies to tell him where he could find a way over the wall to the outside. They led him to a cedar tree, which they explained would bend down upon command and catapult him over the wall if he so desired.

That evening, Fox found the spring where fireflies obtained their water. There, also, he discovered colored earth, which when mixed with water, made paint.[5] He decided to give himself a coat of white.[6] Upon returning to the village, Fox suggested to the fireflies, "Let's have a festival where we can dance and I will produce the music."

(*continued on page 59*)

reason why white-skinned people were first looked upon with amazement by the people of North America. The Native people were soon disappointed and realized that these visitors were not "white light" after all. If fireflies in the story represent white people, and Fox an Apache man, this may also mean that he was pretending to be white as a way of gaining their trust, wearing white man's clothes and speaking the white man's language to them.

7 In most shamanistic cultures, dancing with a drum is a form of prayer, not entertainment. This also implies that the fireflies were whites and not Native Americans, as it is only in white culture that people think of dancing as mere fun and not sacred. Fireflies, like bees, also do a "dance" as a form of communication. The flashing patterns are a means of intelligent communication. There are intertribal social dances where people have fun, but the motto is "All dances are sacred."

8 There are many stories in which the trickster gets the people to imitate him, and then, handing the activity over to them amid great praise, he escapes. Br'er Rabbit, in the Cherokee tales, would not have hesitated to use this device, which is a hallmark of heyokes, harlequins, pranksters, and tricksters of all nations. Mark Twain used this device in *Tom Sawyer* when Tom tricks other boys into whitewashing his fence for him. Twain's mother, a descendent of settlers who had followed Daniel Boone across the mountains through Cherokee country to Kentucky, could well have passed along a few Native American trickster stories she might have heard in her childhood.

9 The sacred cedar symbolizes fire—it is highly flammable and makes for good kindling. Many origin-of-fire stories involve theft, and for theft there is always some sort of Promethean punishment. Fire is a metaphor for any power that has a destructive as well as a helpful side. Knowledge can be such a power and can be misused just as easily as fire, which may be why so many gnostic societies share their knowledge only with initiates. Real foxes today, of course, cannot make or use fire, which "proves" the story is true.

They all agreed that would be fun[7] and helped to gather wood to build up a greater fire. Secretly, Fox tied a piece of cedar bark to his tail. Then he made a drum. According to the Apache elders, this was probably the first one ever constructed, and he beat it vigorously with a stick for the dancing fireflies. Gradually, he moved closer and closer to the fire.

Fox pretended to tire from beating the drum. He gave it to some fireflies who wanted to help make the music.[8] Fox quickly thrust his tail into the fire, lighting the cedar bark, and exclaimed, "It is too warm here for me, I must find a cooler place."

Straight to the cedar tree Fox ran, calling "Bend down cedar tree, bend down!"

The cedar tree bent down for Fox to catch hold, then up it carried him far over the wall. On and on he ran, with the fireflies in pursuit.

As Fox ran along, brush and wood on either side of his path were ignited from the sparks dropping from the burning cedar bark. He brought the burning piece of bark to Hawk, whom the Apache call *itsarltsul*, and Hawk carried it to Brown Crane, whom the Apache call *tsinestsol*. Brown Crane flew far southward, scattering fire sparks everywhere. This is how fire first spread over the earth. Fireflies continued chasing Fox all the way to his burrow and declared, "Forever after, Wily Fox, your punishment for stealing our fire will be that you can never make use of it for yourself."[9] For the Apache tribe, this was the beginning of fire. Soon they learned to use it for cooking their food and to keep themselves warm in cold weather and to help them in their sacred ceremonies.

4
The Sacred Pipe

▤ George A. Dorsey published this story in the *Journal of American Folk Lore* in 1906, with this statement: "The following account of what seems to have been an important tribal ceremony was obtained from Percy Phillips, a young full-blood, educated Sioux, living on the Cheyenne [River] reservation, South Dakota. The pipe referred to in the account is said to belong to the Sans Arcs division of the Teton Sioux [*Itazipčo (Ee-taz-**ip**-tcho)*, "without bows" in Lakota], and is in the possession of Red-Hair, the keeper. The ceremony lasts about half a day and the singing of the ritual is of about one hour's duration." Since 1906, the pipe has changed hands several times and is now believed to be in the possession of Arvol Looking Horse. The word *Sioux* is derived from an Ojibway word meaning "enemy," whereas *Lakota* means "ally."

1 This account seems to have picked up a thread of ancient Dakota lore. It was the Dakota who started out in Minnesota following the buffalo herds westward into the Great Plains. In the Lakota Creation story, according to Tiokasin Ghosthorse, the people lived in an underground cave and emerged at Wind Cave in the western Black Hills, which is where it is believed White Buffalo Calf Woman's pipe was first received, over 2,000 years ago. They then migrated counterclockwise over many centuries and left remnants in South Carolina, southern Ohio, or somewhere in the mountains in between, returning only in recent centuries to the Black Hills.

2 In Black Elk's version of the story, which appears in *The Sacred Pipe*, White Buffalo Calf Woman was carrying a bundle on her back that contained the pipe. As she approached the men, she placed the pipe on the ground before them. Nearly all pipe carriers today carry the pipe in the crook of their left arm, as described here. If the length is standard (just short of a cubit, about twenty inches), the bowl will be in the left hand with the stem tucked into the left crook. When sitting and smoking, the bowl is always held in the left hand as well. The left hand is always used to hold tobacco and cedar and other offerings, as it is directly connected to the heart.

☐ White Buffalo Calf Woman (Lakota)

When the Indians were all living together in the east, near a great lake, they were encamped in a large circle. At that time there was supposed to be but one language spoken; and there were chiefs for every tribe, one chief to every band.[1]

One day, two young men went out hunting in a mountainous country, the Black Hills (on the western side past Bear Butte). At the top of a high tableland they found game. On their way down the hill they saw a woman coming toward them. As they came near to the woman, they noticed that she had something in her arms. On approaching still nearer, they discovered that she was a fine-looking young woman, carrying a pipe on her left arm.[2]

(continued on page 65)

3 The term "outrage" is ambiguous, but later generations presumed it to mean rape, which would fit the story here. However, it could mean to humiliate her sexually in a symbolic way, parallel to the warrior's tradition of "counting coup," either act revealing his base nature.

4 This is the description often used in sacred stories to describe any prophet, man or woman, who is bearing a spiritual gift. It means they are not totally of this world.

5 This is a teaching in itself. Those who are truly on an errand, or a mission from God, do not have time to start fights or cause trouble. As Rev. Martin Luther King Jr. said, "Our eyes are on the prize," which inspired his followers to turn the other cheek again and again.

The Great Medicine is a name for Creator, a term associated mostly with Cheyenne tradition. Its meaning is not so different from *Hashem* (literally, "the name") in the Torah, which connotes "Great Merciful One." "Medicine" does not refer just to physical healing, but to a healing of the heart with love and mercy, a healing of the mind with good information, and a healing of the spirit with wisdom.

6 That the pipe was "packed," filled with tobacco, is highly significant, because many believe that when you hold the packed pipe (on your left arm), your thoughts and prayers are powerful and affect all living things. It is important, therefore, not to entertain anger or jealousy while holding the pipe, which was said to be "more powerful than an atomic bomb" by the late Lakota elder Harry Bird. The one man's unprovoked attack would therefore affect all beings in a disastrous way.

7 The buffalo chip is buffalo dung, "the oil of the plains," which the Lakota used to make fire. As the buffalo is sacred, this has symbolic meaning—the chip is keeping the pipe from touching the earth. It is a clue that this version may have Algonquin roots, either Cheyenne or Blackfoot, since the buffalo chip is central to the Creation story of these peoples. The first woman and her son had just been created. The woman asked Creator whether they would live forever. To decide, Creator tossed a buffalo chip into the river, and of course it floated. "Yes, forever," he said. But the woman insisted on tossing a beautiful stone instead, which sank.

Suddenly, one of the young men said, "Let us outrage her."[3] He tempted the other man, who said, "No, it is not well that you should do anything of the sort, for she is of mysterious appearance."[4] When they came closer, both men stopped and obstructed her way. The woman stopped and said, "I heard what you were saying." The tempter urged his fellow, and said, "Let us leap upon her." The other man answered, "No, you must not harm her." The tempter said, "Yes, I will attack her, for there is no one around." The other man said, "You may, but I will stand aside." The woman said, "I do not wish to stir up any strife, since I am on a special errand from the Great Medicine."[5] With this, she stepped aside, took the pipe, which was seen to be filled,[6] from her left arm and laid it down upon a buffalo chip, with the stem directly toward the east.[7] Then she laughed and sat down. The tempter approached her abruptly, threw her prostrate, and as he was on the verge of outraging her, there seemed to be a very great rumbling in the heavens, and there came forth from the

(continued on page 67)

"There," Old Man said, sadly, "you have chosen. Everything that lives will come to an end."

In the Lakota version told by Black Elk in *The Sacred Pipe*, it is not a buffalo chip but a "stone." However in the ancient Native American way of life, there is little distinction between the secular and sacred spheres of existence, which continues even today among certain traditional elders of the Great Plains. If everything is sacred, certainly buffalo dung, which symbolizes eternal life, is too.

Because the traditional Lakota sweat lodge or *inipi* was arranged with the door facing the rising sun, the pipe would be carried out stem first and then placed in the Y stick of the altar with the stem pointing upward and eastward. Much of this story is meant as ceremonial instruction. Many Lakota sweat lodges face west, and many lodges start at sunset.

8 There is a strange phenomenon called the Ghost Trail that is part of the mystery of the sweat lodge. After the first or second round of the inipi ceremony, the oxygen inside the lodge is used up, and air and smoke from the outside fire are drawn slowly into the lodge. The smoke crawls along the "trail," which is lined in advance with tobacco, and into the lodge. This is especially visible at dusk. Although never specified, it seems to be a manifestation of the Holy Spirit, in Native American terms. It is likely that there is a reference here to the purification ceremony of the inipi lodge, which burns away the impurities of spirit and flesh at the same time. In Black Elk's version, they all become enveloped in a great cloud.

9 The Spirit Land is the world of the afterlife. As in many ancient religious teachings, the spiritual person invests much of his or her time in preparing for the afterlife by resolving their accounts in this one. As Jesus said in the Sermon on the Mount, "Lay up for yourselves treasures in heaven ... " (Matthew 6:20). However, Native Americans are not among those who hold contempt for the physical world, as St. Bernard of Clairvaux did in the Middle Ages. Native people work at making this world more like heaven whenever possible, and that begins with making it colorful and interesting.

heavens as it were, mist that enveloped the place where they lay so that they could not be seen.[8] There they remained for a time, and when the mist lifted there was to be seen only the skeleton of the man, but the woman came away unchanged. The young man who had stood at one side watching was frightened and started to run away, but the woman called him back. As he looked back, the woman told him to go to the camp where all the people were and say, "A sacred pipe is coming to you that will furnish you abundance in the Spirit Land."[9]

(continued on page 69)

10 Dogs, like cats, are highly intuitive and see a person's spirit, according to Native tradition. It's said that dogs only care about what's in your heart.

11 In Black Elk's version, many tipis were hastily taken down and combined to create one large tipi, a communal offering. The chief's name was *Hehlokecha Najin*, Standing Hollow Horn, and White Buffalo Calf Woman had asked for him by name. In that version, she walked around the tipi sunwise (clockwise) and stood in front of Standing Hollow Horn, who would have been at the western end of the tipi, across from the entrance. In Algonquin and Siouian culture, most ceremonies move in clockwise motion to honor Creation; the Thunder Beings work counterclockwise, as they are terrifying and often bring destruction.

A red blanket is often used to carry gifts at a powwow, with six people holding the blanket. It is a nonverbal way of showing honor. The gifts may also be placed upon the blanket on the ground. Red is the sacred color and holds the power of life. It is associated with the east, with the rising sun, with Creator, with our mission in life, and with blood.

12 This part of the speech, which is rather renowned, appears in the Black Elk version of this story and not the Dorsey version.

13 This paragraph and the speech quoted in the next paragraph are also taken from Black Elk's version. In Lakota, *Wakan-Tanka*, "The Great Spirit Who Is One" (the equivalent of Great Mystery), has both a grandfather aspect and a father aspect. Joseph Epes Brown compares the grandfather aspect to the Christian Godhead, and also to Brahma-Nirguna (the formless), and the father aspect to God, or to Brahma-Saguna (Creator, Preserver, Destroyer) in Hinduism (Sanatana Dharma). The familiar *Tunkashila* means "grandfather."

The young man went away as fast as he could, and when he came to the place of the chief he delivered his message. Immediately, all the chiefs were gathered together and they erected a tipi large enough to contain a great many people, and they made ready for the coming of the woman with the pipe. As she appeared on the hilltop on her way to the camp, the lightning flashed in every direction about her. So mysterious was her coming that even the dogs were afraid to bark.[10] As the woman drew near, the chiefs gathered in a circle, holding in their midst a red blanket with a white border; and thus they went forth to meet her. A little distance from the camp, the woman stopped, and when the elders came to her they threw down the blanket for her to stand upon. All of the chiefs took hold of the blanket and carried her to the center of the large tipi especially prepared for her coming.[11]

The woman had with her the large pipe, and when she was set down, she spoke as follows: "This pipe is to be transmitted from generation to generation, and thus it shall be handed down to the end of time."[12]

She held the pipe before the chief and said, "Behold this and always love it! It is *lila wakan*, very sacred, and you must treat it as such. No impure man should ever be allowed to see it, for within this bundle there is a sacred pipe. With this you will, during the winters to come, send your voices to *Wakan-Tanka* [Great Mystery], your Father and Grandfather."[13]

The woman laid the pipe on a buffalo chip. Again she spoke, and said: "With this sacred pipe you will walk upon the Earth, for the Earth is your Grandmother and Mother, *Maka*, and she is sacred. Every step that is taken upon her should be as a prayer. The bowl of this pipe is of red stone; it is the Earth. Carved in the stone and facing

(continued on page 71)

14 There is no reason to think that this was the first pipe, or that earlier pipes were not sacred. In fact, everyone in the story seems to know what a pipe is, however, *this* pipe is one of great strength. Its large size is a visual clue as to its inner power. Other pipes are connected to particular ancestors and other beings in the spirit world, but this pipe is connected to Creator through White Buffalo Calf Woman. Joseph Epes Brown says Spotted Eagle flies the highest and is the solar bird. He also mentions that the eagle is associated with the mind, similar to the Buddhi, the formless, transcendent principle of the intellect in Hindu tradition. Many Native American medicine men, including the Lakota, use the eagle bone to make a flute, which makes a high, single-toned whistle sound, heard in the sweat lodge. This note is identical to the esoteric sound that devotees of Sikhism wish to hear during their multi-dimensional journeys toward the Godhead, and they refer to it as the voice of God in one of its purest manifestations. Sufis and Kabirites hear the same sound and meditate on it. The Scythians of the Ukraine, who lived 2,500 years ago, also used the bones of eagles to make flutes.

15 The pipe is not smoked all the time, or just for fun. It is always smoked for a good purpose, when someone requests it and gives the appropriate offering in the traditional manner. The speech about "one nation" might be interpreted to mean that the sacred *chanupa tehinsela* (the pipe of White Buffalo Calf Woman) was sent to unite all the Native American nations. This has not happened quite yet!

16 The pipe was not worshiped as a deity, so this may be the storyteller's own embellishment, or a mistranslation from the Lakota. It suggests a hierarchical system, which is not typical of pre-Christian Lakota cosmologies. The Sacred Pipe is a direct link to the supreme deity, as are all awakened pipes, to some extent, through the ancestors. Incidents of real idolatry are rare in Native American lore; however many objects are manifestations of the divine, and are "transparent to the transcendent," as Joseph Campbell would say. It is said that the stem represents the people or the male, and the stone bowl represents the earth or

the center is this buffalo calf who represents all the four-leggeds who live upon your Mother. The stem of the pipe is of wood, and this represents all that grows upon the Earth. And these twelve feathers which hang here where the stem fits into the bowl are from *Wanbli Gleska*, Spotted Eagle, and they represent the eagle and all the wingeds of the air. All these peoples and all the things of the universe are joined to you who smoke the pipe—all send their voices to Wakan-Tanka, the Great Spirit. When you pray with this pipe, you pray for and with everything![14]

"There shall be but one nation, and by that nation this pipe must be kept sacred; it must be used in time of war, in time of famine, in time of sickness, in time of need of any sort as an instrument for preservation.[15] This pipe will be your chief deity.[16] It must be kept by the best chief of the tribe, and must be attended to once a year by the assemblage of the most upright chiefs. Whenever they open

(continued on page 73)

the female; when the earth and the people are connected, miracles happen, and Creation continues.

17 Traditional tampers I have seen are made from pieces of wood, roots, or branches, over a quarter inch thick and two inches long, whittled and tapered at one end to tamp down the tobacco.

18 A separate book could be written about the controversies surrounding what some have called "the most sacred object in North America." It seems possible that Dorsey mixed together the descriptions of two pipes: one pipe made from red pipestone with a carved buffalo calf figure (which the majority of people believe is held by Arvol Looking Horse), and another one carved from buffalo bones (others say cottonwood) and not designed to be smoked, to which the ear and hair were attached. Perhaps this is the one White Buffalo Calf Woman instructed the people to make. In 1906, when the Phillips account was first published, the pipe had already been passed from Red Hair to Elk Head, Sr. His descendant, Hannah Elk Head Red Horse, saw the ear-adorned pipe around 1934, and Frank Fools Crow claimed he once saw the pipe with the ear still attached in 1976 but did not reveal who held it at that time. There were also seven council pipes made from caitlinite, or red pipestone.

The pipe carrier's way is to trust that Creator will provide to those in his service, and although the pipe carrier gives away what he has to those in need, he "walks in balance upon the earth" with power and dignity. This non-ownership is central to Native American society, but still difficult to achieve. The pipe carrier at times will hold the pipe up to heaven with both hands saying, "Creator, this is your pipe. If in your eyes I am not worthy to hold it, take it from me!"—knowing that Creator just might!

19 The pipe in this regard is similar to the Water Babies, water guardians of the Washo, but also like the tribal angels of Israel, and the wrathful protector deities of Tibet. They are powerful allies to the righteous, but deadly enemies to wayward mortals.

the pipe there must be made tools expressly for handling the fire: a certain stick must be trimmed and handled by virgins or by young men of chastity, expressly for the pipe; a tamper;[17] and a little spoon must be made to take up the fire. The pipe must have a wrapping of wool of the buffalo only. From the first enemy that shall be killed through the power of the pipe, an ear shall be cut off and tied to the pipe stem. The first scalp to be taken shall be treated in the same way. Whenever you are hungry, my instructions must be followed. Ten men shall open the pipe, to plead to the Great Owner of the pipe.[18] Should the man holding the pipe do any wrong, there would be a demolition of his whole family.[19] Through the advice of your ten best chiefs the pipe shall be kept by the very best chief of all. As long as the holder shall walk reverently and keep himself in order, the keeping of the pipe shall be hereditary."

As the woman was leaving the tipi, she said that she was going to stop four times on the way to the hill, and the ten chiefs should smoke the pipe as she was leaving, and that the fourth time, she would stop and transform herself into four colors, of the four directions. The ten chiefs lighted the pipe, and as they were smoking,

(*continued on page 75*)

20 Many believe that as she turned into a buffalo, she rolled four times on the ground, changing from white, to red, to yellow, to black, and then returning to white, symbolizing the four races of humankind and the four directions.

The following public statement is from Gloria Hazell of Pipestone, Minnesota: "Ten years ago a small buffalo was born, she was a sign to Native Americans and those who follow the Red Road worldwide, she was a sign of hope for the world, she was a sign that at last we may have peace on earth. She was Miracle the White Buffalo. She was born in Wisconsin, to a pair of ordinary brown buffalo. There had been a prophesy that a white buffalo would be born that would herald the return of the White Buffalo Calf Woman, the entity who brought the sacred red Chanupa (Pipe) to the Lakota People. The White Buffalo Calf Woman had promised that she would return one day, and it was thought that this tiny white Buffalo was this promise fulfilled. The prophecy said that the father of this buffalo would die of natural causes within a couple of months of the birth, that way no other calf could be born from these parents. True to the prophecy the father, Marvin, did die of natural causes about a month after Miracle was born. As Miracle grew her color changed; she went from white to yellow to red to black and then to brown. At that point people said that she had started to go back to white again, but because the world wasn't ready for her she stayed brown. The White Buffalo Calf Woman had changed color as she left the Lakota people, first she turned into a buffalo and then she lay down, turned over, and over and changed into all of the same colors that Miracle did, the colors of mankind."

Black Elk, in *The Sacred Pipe*, states, "White Buffalo Cow Woman who brought our sacred pipe will appear again at the end of this 'world,' a coming which we Indians know is now not very far off."

21 This refers to a woman on her "moon time." At the full moon, a woman menstruates, and this is sometimes referred to as "unclean." The heat energy emanating from a woman on her moon is not harmful to women but is believed to be draining for men, so the women spend the time in the moon lodge together, praying to *unči maka ina*

the woman went away, then stopped and looked back. Again she went on, and looked back. Again she stopped and looked back, and the fourth time she stopped and looked back, she turned toward the hill and ran, and she transformed herself into a splendid five-year-old buffalo, then disappeared in the hills.[20]

Now the chiefs assembled and held a council so as to establish rules regulating the keeping of the pipe. They selected the best chief to hold the pipe. During the ceremony of the pipe, he was to relate exactly the story that the woman had told when she brought the pipe to the camp and was not to deviate from or leave out any of her words. While the chiefs were still in council, they secured a wrapper for the pipe, also all the sticks that were necessary for use with the pipe, all made by maidens. The pipe was then raised high aloft in the midst of the council lodge. The pipe was cared for with great reverence. No unclean woman might approach it.[21]

(continued on page 77)

(*oon-tchee ma-ka een-a*) loosely, "Grandmother/Mother Earth." The "bloods" purifies the women very effectively. It is said that as long as a women experiences menstruation, she does not need to go into a sweat lodge or to do fasting to be purified, because "it's taken care of." Because of the toxins and earth energies being tossed off at that time, women are not to touch the pipe or go into the sweat lodge.

22 According to Dorsey, "The [sacred] pipe when not in use is kept in a bundle which is about three feet long; the pipe itself being protected by gifts or offerings which have been made to it, then wrapped with buckskin and placed in a bag of woven buffalo hair. The outer wrapper of buffalo hide has been replaced by one of canvas. The ceremony is said to be performed in influential families when a girl first attains the age of womanhood and also when a period of mourning is stopped by a formal feast." It is said that the buffalo's secret is in his hair, particularly his beard. Hair holds the spiritual power for humans as well as for the buffalo; and the beard is a symbol of grandfatherhood. Some stories even say his beard is the hair of humans he has eaten. In the best-known version of the story, the hair turned the four colors of the four directions, which represents wholeness, or accepting the universe as it is. Some believe the pipe is two thousand years old, whereas Dorsey suggests it is nine hundred.

23 Although the term "peace pipe" is something of a stereotype (along with the phrase "smokum peace-pipe" and other insulting doggerel), certain tribes and nations have used a pipe of peace for centuries. The Algonquin path to peace known as the Way of the Heron includes extensive customs for resolving conflicts, such as the peace pipe ceremony, which were well documented in colonial times and adopted by whites.

24 The sharing of a "pipe of peace" was an essential part of the conflict resolution process, as it was understood that to "smoke on it" and then lie would be to invite disaster or death. Truth-telling is an essential part of living a happy, peaceful life.

A few days after the pipe had been brought, there was a quarrel within the camp in which two people were killed. In accordance with the woman's command, they cut the ear from one and tied it on the pipe stem, together with the scalp, and that ear and that scalp are on that pipe to this day. The same sticks that were made by the ancient people as well as the covering of buffalo hair, are still with the ancient pipe, which is said to be nine hundred years old.[22]

This pipe is now kept by an old Sioux chief who lives at the Cheyenne [River] Agency, South Dakota, and who is about ninety-three years old.

There have been offerings made to this pipe by different tribes, such as bracelets, earrings, rings, arrows, brushes, stones, and various other trinkets being given to the pipe alone, all of which are kept with the pipe. They say that whenever in need or hungry, the buffalo gone, they go to work and call the ten best men in, who go and plead to the pipe, having unwrapped it, and that within one to three days thereafter, they receive all that they had prayed for. Since the scattering of the tribe, in times of peace, the pipe is held as peacemaker, and hence is sometimes called "the pipe of peace,"[23] but the people call it the "calf pipe," for the woman who brought it transformed herself into a buffalo, and the pipe coming from her must therefore be a calf.

General Custer swore by this pipe that he was not going to fight the Indians anymore. But the very next summer, he met death, for he disregarded the oath he had made to the pipe.[24] He who swears by the pipe and breaks the oath comes to destruction, and his whole family dies, or sickness comes upon them.

5
"Why?"
Stories

1 In Eastern Woodland cultures as far north as New England, to "wear the buckhorns" was to be the leader, the chief, or *sachem.* Among animals and inanimate objects, the largest of the species was called "the chief." The moose was the chief of the northern forest, the whale was the chief of the ocean, and the eagle the chief of raptors. The peak of rocks known today as Sam's Point in the Shawangunks of the Catskill Range was called *Ioskawasting,* which means, "it wears the buckhorns from across the way." The tallest peak, though very unassuming from close up, stands out from a hundred miles away in every direction.

Each animal in Native American culture symbolically has two sides, a positive and a negative side, a light and a dark side. There is a time for each, but generally we try to reflect the positive in our own lives.

In this story, we see these two opposite kinds of leaders, evenly matched, and entering into a contest of endurance to see who will "wear the buckhorns." In Native democracies, local chiefs often had to run for election, based on their widely varying styles of problem-solving. A chief who is a quick thinker and resourceful (in other words, a rabbit) was respected as long as he could be trusted. A chief who was of noble character, who sacrificed himself for the people (a deer), was considered the ideal, as long as he was decisive. On one level, this story is obviously about an election for chief between two opposite kinds of people, a rabbit type and a deer type. The antlers represent the crown of tribal authority.

In Native spiritual teaching, we are all just ordinary people. We are all equal. When someone is acting out his or her role in office, as a healer, chief, or medicine man, that person has been formally invited to serve in that way. In some Cherokee traditions, a true healer or *shaman* can only be chosen by Creator, and only after being struck by lightning can one be called truly chosen. I've heard it said by a Cherokee elder, "If you want to be calling yourself a Medicine Man in my tribe, you'd better have been hit at least two or three times by lightning!" Even in that case, it is only after being asked that you enter into the role. When the chief wears the buckhorns, his position is to be

☐ How Deer Got His Horns (Cherokee)

In the beginning, Deer had no horns at all. His head was smooth like the doe. He was a great runner, but Rabbit was a great jumper. Both covered a lot of ground, but by different means. All of the other animals were eager to know which one could go farther in the same amount of time. This became a regular topic of conversation at gatherings and the source of more than a few wagers. At last, they arranged a contest between Deer and Rabbit. They created a nice pair of antlers as a prize for the winner. Deer and Rabbit were to start together from one side of a thicket, go through the thicket, then turn around and come back. The one who made it back first to the finish line would wear the horns on his head. Then all the people would know he was the best—the strongest runner and jumper.[1]

On the day of the match, all of the animals showed up to see who would win. The antlers were laid on the ground at the edge of the thicket to mark the starting point. While everybody was admiring the horns, Rabbit said, "I don't know this part of the country. I'll ... just ... kinda ... take a *look* through these bushes where we are going to run."

(continued on page 83)

respected, as he represents the entire tribe or nation's interests. To kill him is to enter into a debt with every citizen of that nation. However, when he removes the antlers, he is like everyone else. This story is a test to see which of these "people" will wear the crown.

2 Rabbit has turned to his dark side as trickster and is caught cheating. He is not using his brains and talent for the good of the people but is only looking out for himself. As the philosopher Kant points out, there is no virtue in genius if it is not motivated by good will. This is a key to Eastern Woodland philosophy, which like the samurai, sees the mind as a good servant but a terrible master. "Don't think so much!" is a common expression. "Let your mind be like a clear pond" is another. The Cherokee say, "Listen with your heart, not just your ears." They also say, "Be truthful at all times and under all conditions."

This story also shows us something of the rabbit's habits; he likes to gnaw on branches and run around in the thicket.

3 The Cherokee say, "To serve others, to be of some use to family, community, Nation, and the world, is one of the main purposes for which human beings have been created…. True happiness comes only to those who dedicate their lives to the service of others." The ending of the story lets us know that the type of person who is of noble and dignified character, who sacrifices himself for others, is a much better leader in the long run than the one who is quick-thinking and resourceful. It is he who should "wear the buckhorns." The fact that in nature the deer does indeed wear the horns becomes an illustration of the truth of these teachings. "See?" the elders would say. "It's true!" According to Brian Wilkes, director of the Standing Bear Foundation, the Cherokee have "day signs" rather than sun signs, and Rabbit and Deer are adjacent to each other. Rabbit, or "Big Star," is the planet Venus, while "Little Deer" is the head of Taurus, minus the Pleiades. It is said that the only time Rabbit can ever wear Deer's antlers is when Venus passes through Taurus, which would be once in a blue moon, so to speak.

The animals thought it was all right. So Rabbit went into the thicket. But he was gone so long that, at last, the animals suspected he must be up to one of his tricks. They sent a messenger to look for him. The messenger found him, away in the middle of the thicket, gnawing a tunnel through the bushes and pulling them away until he had a road cleared nearly to the other side.[2]

The messenger turned around quietly and came back and told the other animals. When Rabbit came out of the thicket, they accused him of cheating. He denied it, until they went into the thicket and found the cleared road. They agreed that such a trickster had no right to enter the race at all. So they gave the horns to Deer, who was named the best runner, and he has worn them ever since. They told Rabbit that, as he was so fond of cutting down bushes, he might consider doing that for a living—and so he does to this day.[3]

1 This is the second part of the same story. It gives us more insight into the interdependent texture of real life, both spiritually and politically.

2 There is a balance of all things in the natural world; when losers are not given a consolation prize (or some sense of inclusion), there will be a reckoning, because everyone deserves respect. It is considered wise for the winner to be humble in victory so as to avoid the wrath of the losers, and to help build what Native leaders have always sought: consensus. If one party is angry, they will scheme to disrupt consensus, so that the people are not of one mind. The Cherokee say, "The hurt of one is the hurt of all. The honor of one is the honor of all." It is also said, "Observe moderation and balance in all things." This search for balance in all things pervades every corner of Native American life; it is what people today call eco-wisdom, but it was not made up retroactively after scientists "discovered" ecology. This type of dynamic balance has been the cornerstone of Native wisdom teaching for thousands of years.

Most children's stories end as soon as there is a winner. But there is always a loser, too, and they have their side of the story to tell. In this part of the story, there is a striving for reciprocity, or balance. We *want* to just hear about the winner, but this story trains us to hear both sides. In Native teaching, we never shut anyone out of our lives; we live in an eternal circle of life where there is no word for good-bye (indeed "good-bye" does not exist in any Algonkian or Lakota language, only "see you again"). Nothing is ever really over. Stephen Sondheim illustrates this in the Broadway show *Into the Woods*, where he tells us about the hardship that Jack of beanstalk fame caused the poor giant's wife after he slew the giant—a very Native American twist on things.

3 We also see portrayed here a great truth: that excellence attracts jealousy, and not knowing how to handle jealousy can be the downfall of a great leader in any field. Jealousy is best dealt with by cautious, gradual power-sharing in the Native tradition, not with naivete or hostility. The deer's dark side is that he is too naive, too idealistic, and as leader he is tested again and again until he learns that not all beings are

Why Deer's Teeth Are Blunt
(Cherokee)

Rabbit was angry because Deer had won the horns on the day the two raced.[1] So Rabbit planned to get even.[2]

One day, soon after the race, Rabbit stretched a large grapevine across the trail and gnawed it nearly in two in the middle. Then he went back a little way, took a good run, and jumped up the vine, until Deer came along and asked him what he was doing.

"Don't you see?" said Rabbit. "I'm so strong I can bite through that grapevine at one jump."

Deer could hardly believe this, and wanted to see it done. So Rabbit ran back, made a tremendous spring and bit through the vine where he had gnawed it before. Deer, when he saw that, said, "Well, if you can do it, I can too."[3]

So Rabbit stretched another thick grapevine across the trail—but without gnawing it in the middle. Deer ran back, as he had seen Rabbit do, made a spring and struck the grapevine right in the middle. But the vine only flew back, and threw him over on his head. He tried again and again until he was bruised and bleeding.

"Let me see your teeth," Rabbit said at last. Deer showed Rabbit his teeth, which were long like a wolf's teeth, but not very sharp.

(continued on page 87)

as enlightened as he is. Apparently this is one of the first tests. He must, like any martyr figure, either take every challenge to his crown and be bruised and beaten, or learn how to say, "No, not today. Let's just take it easy." He should take off his crown of office and be an "ordinary person," in this case, and not be damaged by foolish wagers.

4 A deer person is not very competitive, but at least he can speak the truth, such as the harangue (a traditional Native art of criticizing and making complaint), and therefore "have some teeth." This rabbit is very competitive, and must find a way to dull the edge of Deer's criticism in the future, and thereby—so he hopes—regain his own stature. The term "rabbit-ears" means someone is thin-skinned and doesn't like criticism. Many Native terms for rabbit translate to the same thing, "his ears are close together," which indicates a person will have trouble hearing both sides of the story.

5 Of course the dark side of Deer is that he is altogether too willing to endure suffering for the sake of right, and too willing to keep quiet, and Rabbit, being a trickster, can see his weaknesses as if they were painted on his face. Such is the way of most con artists; all they need is to be given the benefit of the doubt.

6 The phrase "Now you've paid for your horns" is a classic line. Substitute "crown" for "horns" and it is equal to any line from Shakespeare, and it speaks volumes about the human condition.

A child who is known to cheat will be told this story with a great deal of emphasis on how "that bad rabbit" caused all this trouble. A child who is too naive and gullible will be told this story with great emphasis on how Deer brought on this trouble by trusting wily Rabbit too much. Neither is the right version or the wrong version. As I have been told, "The Mi'kmaq didn't have jails or mental institutions, they had *ahdooga'an*" (teaching tales). When people are raised right on strong stories, they grow up strong, ready to deal with small problems before they get big. That way, tyranny never gets a foothold.

"No wonder you can't do it," sighed the tricky Rabbit. "Your teeth are too blunt to bite anything. Let me *sharpen* them for you, like mine! Ha ha ha! My teeth are so sharp that I can cut through a stick better than you can with a knife."[4]

He showed Deer a black locust twig that, in rabbit fashion, he had shaved off as well as a knife. Deer thought Rabbit's idea was good. So Rabbit got a hard stone with rough edges and filed and filed at Deer's teeth, until they were worn down almost to the gums.

"It hurts," said Deer. But Rabbit said, "Oh, it always hurts a little when the teeth begin to get sharp." So Deer kept quiet.[5]

After much filing, Rabbit said, "Now try to bite the vine." Deer tried again, but this time he could not bite at all.

"Now you've paid for your horns," said Rabbit, as he jumped away through the bushes.[6]

Ever since then, Deer's teeth have been so blunt that he cannot chew through anything but grass and leaves.

I will end by saying that both Deer and Rabbit were very sorry for their mistakes, and tried to do better next time.

▤ The opening and closing sections about Muskrat and War Eagle are not traditional, but are from Frank B. Linderman's version of this story, published in 1915.

1 The teaching that small beings can be the greatest allies is one of the most prevalent themes in Native American stories of all nations. In a society that places a premium on physical survival, and therefore strength, it is important to remember that the small and meek often end up being critical players. It also shows how stories can instill an ethical system into a society in subtle ways, ensuring equality, justice, mercy, and tolerance. Actions are of tantamount importance in Native life, but might does not make right in any case. The term "mice-people" reflects a Native American tendency in English to use "people" to refer to any species.

2 This is another form of Coyote Old Man, called *Wateo* by the Cheyenne. He has a playful, tricky side sometimes, and a side that is indifferent to human problems, but beneath it all, it is said he is the Creator of the universe.

☐ Why the Blackfeet Never Kill Mice
(Blackfeet/Ojibway)

A boy named Muskrat and his grandmother were gathering wood for the camp, when they came to an old buffalo skull. The plains were dotted with these relics of the chase, for already the hide-hunting white man had played havoc with the great herds of buffalo. This skull was in a grove of cottonwood trees near the river, and, as they approached, two mice scampered into it to hide. Muskrat, in great glee, secured a stick and was about to turn the skull over and kill the mice, when his grandmother said, "No, our people never kill mice. Your grandfather will tell you why if you ask him. The mice-people are our friends and we treat them as such. Even small people can be good friends, you know—remember that."[1]

All the day, the boy wondered why the mice-people should not be harmed, and just at dark he came to his grandfather War Eagle's lodge. He intended to ask for the reason as soon as he arrived. He found the other children already there, and, almost before he sat down, Muskrat asked, "Grandfather, why must we never kill the mice-people? Grandmother said that you knew."

"Yes," replied War Eagle, "I do know and you must know. Therefore I shall tell you all tonight why the mice-people must be let alone and allowed to do as they please, for we owe them much much more than we can ever pay. Yes—they are great people, as you will see.

"It happened long, long ago, when there were few men and women in the world. Old Man was chief of all then,[2] and the animal-people and the bird-people were greater than our people, because we had not been on earth long and were not wise.

(continued on page 91)

3 As with many stories for children's ears, this one starts with a quarrel. It seems as though children can be stopped from quarreling among one another if they can be distracted long enough to forget the purpose of their quarrel. This story would serve as a nice distraction from such a fight. Too bad world leaders can't be told stories until they forget why they are fighting. Within the story, of course, the distraction is the ancient hand bone game, which has many names in the Native world.

4 Many tribes have played the hand bone game, perhaps for thousands of years. This game is designed to improve the intuition of future hunters, as they must "hunt" for the bone of a game animal in the other players' hands. It is said to be a method for developing second sight—a form of seeing in which animals excel, one that is poised between the inner and outer worlds—not to mention quick thinking and mindfulness of small and fleeting clues and signs. Some versions of the game are incredibly complex, with a special scoring board in which marking sticks of different colors can be inserted. The authentic hand game, or bone game, involves four sticks or bones, not one. After the pointer points, the other two players dramatically open their four hands, revealing the location of the bones.

5 Usually, there is gambling or some kind of wager or stakes involved with this game. When used to prevent all-out war, the stakes are high, as the stakes of war are even higher. In this story what is at stake is nothing less than the leadership of the world as it was known then to the animals.

"There was much quarreling among the animals and the birds. You see, Bear wanted to be chief, under Old Man, and so did Beaver. Almost every night they would have a council and quarrel over it. Beside Bear and Beaver there were other animals, and also birds, who thought they had the right to be chief. They couldn't agree and the quarreling grew worse as time went on.[3] Some said the swiftest traveler should be chosen. Others said the greatest chief should be the leader. Others thought the wisest one was the one they wanted. So it went on and on until they were all enemies instead of friends, and you could hear them quarreling almost every night, until Old Man came along that way.

"He heard about the trouble. I forget who told him, but I think it was Rabbit. Anyhow, he visited the council where the quarreling was going on and listened to what each one had to say. It took until almost daylight, too. He listened to it all—every bit. When they had finished talking and the quarreling commenced as usual, he said, 'Stop,' and they did stop.

"Then he said to them, 'I will settle this thing right here and right now, so that there will be no more rows over it, forever.'

"He opened his paint sack and took from it a small, polished bone. This he held up in the firelight, so that they might all see it, and he said:

"'This will settle the quarrel. You all see this bone in my right hand, don't you?'

"'Yes,' they all replied.

"'Well, now you watch the bone and my hands, too, for they are quick and cunning.'[4]

"Old Man began to sing the gambling song and to slip the bone from one hand to the other so rapidly and smoothly that they were all puzzled. Finally he stopped singing and held out his hands—both shut tight, and both with their backs up.

"'Which of my hands holds the bone now?' he asked them.[5]

(continued on page 93)

6 | The quickness of mind and the attention to detail that mice possess is legendary, not only throughout Native American tribes and nations, but around the world. It shows that these qualities are not just useful in urban office surroundings, but in traditional life, as well. The mouse is clearly the hero of this story. Although Buffalo, Bear, and Rabbit are great power animals in other ways, no animal can match the mouse for its attention to detail, its quickness, sharp eyes, and intuitive ability. This story reminds us that the first shall be made last, the last first, that the least of these shall become great, and that Creator loves us all, great and small, equally.

"Some said it was in the right hand, and others claimed that it was the left hand that held it. Old Man asked Bear to name the hand that held the bone, and Bear did, but when Old Man opened that hand it was empty—the bone was not there. Then everybody laughed at Bear. Old Man smiled a little and began to sing and again pass the bone.

"'Beaver, you are smart; name the hand that holds the bone this time.'

"Beaver said: 'It's in your right hand. I saw you put it there.'

"Old Man opened that hand right before the beaver's eyes, but the bone wasn't there, and again everybody laughed—especially Bear.

"'Now, you see,' said Old Man, 'that this is not as easy as it looks, but I am going to teach you all to play the game; and when you have all learned it, you must play it until you find out who is the cleverest at the playing. Whoever that is, he shall be chief under me, forever.'

"Some were awkward and said they didn't care much who was chief, but all of them learned to play pretty well. First Bear and Beaver tried it, but Beaver beat Bear easily and held the bone for a long time. Finally Buffalo beat Beaver and started to play with Mouse. Of course Mouse had small hands and was quicker than Buffalo—quicker to see the bone.[6] Buffalo tried hard for he didn't want Mouse to be chief, but it didn't do him any good, for Mouse won in the end.

(continued on page 95)

7 This little hero is unlike the mouse in "The Mouse and the Lion" from Aesop's fables, who is so taken with his own success that he insists on marrying the Lion King's daughter as promised, only to be crushed when she trips while walking down the aisle with him. This truly gallant mouse wins the chieftaincy through his principal ability, paying intuitive attention to detail, but he wisely declines the position and turns it over to humankind (which some may say was *not* so wise a thing to do).

8 A story is best told with some kind of prop or visual aid, and many stories are designed to get the most dramatic use out of a common household object, such as a child's toy bow and arrow, a peach pit game set, a squash, a turtle shell, or a bone game set. Like mice, children are small and attentive to detail. A good bone game player might be able to keep the children guessing for a while, but then if one guessed correctly, the storyteller could say, "*Ha!* I think we have a little mouse here!"

"It was a fair game and Mouse was chief under the agreement. He looked quite small among the rest but he walked confidently out to the center of the council and said, in a small but commanding voice: 'Listen, brothers—what is mine to keep is mine to give away. I am too small to be your chief and I know it. I am not warlike. I want to live in peace with my wife and family. I know nothing of war. I get my living easily. I don't like to have enemies. I am going to give my right to be chief to Man. Let humankind have all the worry and strife and responsibility. As for me, I choose the simple life.'[7]

"You saw the mice run into the buffalo skull, of course. This is where they have lived and brought up their families ever since the night Mouse beat Buffalo playing the bone game. Yes—the mice people always make their nests in the heads of the dead buffalo-people, ever since that night.

"Our people play the same game, even today. See … " and War Eagle took from his paint sack a small, polished bone. Then he sang, just as Old Man did. He let the children try to guess the hand that held the bone, as the animal-people did that fateful night; but, like the animals, they always guessed wrong.[8]

6
The Sacred Hero

≣ Although this story has several elements from the Navajo tale "Twin Warriors Atone with Their Father," including the pipe-smoking test, and although Man-Eagle has much in common with Dark Father of that story, this is not just a father-son saga like *Oedipus Rex*. It is a variation on the universal myth of the eternal triangle: the rivalry for the love of a woman between an older man of worldly power and a fair-faced younger man, one who is poor but who wins the heart of the beloved with his heroism.

1 In another version of the story, Man-Eagle laid waste "over all the earth. He preyed upon the Hopi, Tewa, Zuni, Navaho, Yoche, Yu'ta, Pa'yutse, Kohonina, and all peoples." There are several layers of meaning to this story. On one level, we take it at face value: it is a story about the hero's journey as he battles a stock villain. On another, it suggests a son confronting and overthrowing an aspect of his father, the way Zeus overthrew Chronos. On another very interesting layer, it is about the return of the sun around Beltane, May 1. Man-Eagle is associated with winter, the season that has laid waste to the entire country, and Son of Light is like the springtime sun, quickening the pulse of the earth goddess.

2 The biting cold of winter wind is personified here in the eagle's sharp talons. The young solar prince must liberate the Goddess of the Land from the binds of his rival and caress her with his warmth, glorifying her fertility. On perhaps the most important level, the story is about taming the destructive forces of nature. The transformation of Man-Eagle into a human at the end of the story underscores this interpretation.

3 Stories of abductions of women by evil aliens are quite common. Many of the stories in the anthology *Grandmother Spider* by Paula Gunn Allen are of this type, representing a spiritual crisis within the family, one of alienation between men and women. Discussing the abuses imposed on the women by the aliens is a way of inquiring into the listener's own issues without being intrusive. The four days and nights of abuse represent the months when the solar prince must live in exile in the south, or in the outer world.

☐ Son of Light Defeats the Monster
(Hopi)

A terrible monster named *Kwa'toko* (Man-Eagle) was laying waste to the entire country.[1] He seized women and girls, wives and maidens with his sharp talons and abducted them.[2] He flew off with them to his home above the clouds, where he punished and abused them for four days and nights before eating them up.[3]

(continued on page 101)

4 Stories from the Welsh classic the *Mabinogion*—in which we find the Flower Maiden Olwen and the eternally young Culwch—follow this same universal pattern.

5 Symbolically, the threat on her life is an illusion. Son of Light is jealous of his rival, and so thinks that she is being harmed by him, as a visitor to the north from the sunny south might imagine that winter is destroying the earth. The Piñon maidens' grass skirts represent the grass at the foot of a pine tree in the spring, and the maidens are similar to Hammadryads in Greek myth, or the Wood Nymphs of widespread European fame.

6 Son of Light is not yet a mature ruler because he "has no armor" (i.e., he is too trusting and leaves himself open to attack) and is too naive and foolish to know that he needs some. He is what Robert Bly calls a *puer aeternus,* the "eternal child." Man-Eagle, a chief, is very good at self-preservation and has a shirt of flint. In other words, he has developed a tough exterior. There is a Native American expression that a chief must have "seven layers of skin" to be a good chief. The idea of an item of flint belonging to a supreme ruler is found throughout the world; for example, the "Cask of Flint" in the Rynd Papyrus is the sarcophagus of the great Pharaoh. Flint, also known as rhyolite or firestone, is one of the hardest of stones and is difficult to carve. Its value was recognized long before gold's, as it can be used as a striker to make fire. A leader must have a hard side to make hard decisions, as well as a gentle side to protect the weak. The shirt of flint reminds me of the "Ghost Shirt" of the Lakota, which is said to deflect bullets, and also of the Mayomi shirt—the "prayer" or "ribbon" shirt worn by Eastern Woodlands people—which is said to protect the pipe carrier from bad medicine.

Among those abducted by Man-Eagle was the young wife of Son of Light.[4] Soon, this hero was in pursuit. Along the way, at the foot of the San Francisco Mountains, he met the Piñon Maidens dressed in grass skirts and piñon-bark mantles. Standing around with them were Spider Woman and Mole Man.

"Where are you going?" they asked.

"Kwa'toko (Man-Eagle) has stolen my wife," he answered. "I am going to rescue her, but I have to get there in a hurry; I'm sure he will kill her very soon!"[5]

"This is bad," said Spider Woman. "But have no fear. I'll help you!" To the Piñon Maidens, she said, "You girls gather piñon resin and shape it into a replica of Man-Eagle's shirt of flint (*yo'ishivwa na'bna*), made of hundreds of arrowheads that no weapon can penetrate. But hurry!"[6]

(*continued on page 103*)

7 The magic corn pollen represents the fertility of the land in spring-time. Corn is used by the Hopi and other Southwest peoples, as well as the Cherokee, Shawnee, and Iroquois people, as an offering, similar to the way tobacco is used by the Lakota, Iroquois/Haudenosaunee, and Algonquins. The practice of smoking tobacco came to the Northeast only about 1000 B.C.E., but tobacco goes back to the dawn of time, sprinkled as a blessing, and is therefore often mentioned in Creation stories, as is corn, which actually came much later in history.

8 Although she is invisible to Son of Light, the voice of Spider Woman can be clearly heard whispering into his right ear. This is an esoteric teaching concerning the way that we are supposed to hear the voice of the Great Spirit, and certain other guiding deities, as a whisper in the right ear, although we cannot see them. They are, in a sense, "inside us" too, weaving the worlds together.

The grain of salt, as a tiny "rock," represents the entire earth, but also the smallest common denominator. The teaching is that all the power of the earth lies within the smallest stone, just as all the spirit power of the ocean lies within a single drop of water, and all the power of air lies within the smallest feather. By the same token, all the power of humanity lies within the least of us, and we are like the "tiny but all-powerful warrior" talked of in certain Iroquois stories. We just have to have faith.

9 Another reason Son of Light is not yet worthy to be chief is that he does not know how to be cunning, how to hide himself. Mole Man takes care of that for him. Here we learn that Man-Eagle lives in the clouds. Could it be he is the sun and, therefore, the father of Son of Light? We don't know, but mythopoetically, a young man competing with a much older man for a woman is subconsciously doing battle with his father for his mother's love.

10 Spotted Eagle is mentioned in *The Sacred Pipe* as representative of the higher mind. Joseph Epes Brown writes that the spotted eagle flies the highest, and yet in this Hopi story, Spotted Eagle is the lowest of the

The Piñon Maidens gathered the resin and made a shirt exactly like Man-Eagle's. They washed it so that Kwa'toko might not detect the imitation by its smell. And when they had finished, Spider Woman sprinkled sacred corn pollen over it and chanted an invocation.[7] She gave the boy some of her special medicine, in the form of cornmeal. Then she shrunk herself into a tiny spider no bigger than a grain of salt and crawled up into Son of Light's right ear.[8] "Here I am," she said, "in your right ear, where I can tell you what to do in case you get into trouble. The next step is up to Mole Man."

Mole Man burrowed a passage through the mountain up to the top so that Son of Light could get to the top without being seen.[9] When they came out onto the mountaintop, they saw that they were still far below Man-Eagle's home in the clouds. Spider Woman said, "I'll just call on some good-hearted birds to help us!"

The first to answer her call was Spotted Eagle.[10] Son of Light, Mole Man, and Spider Woman climbed onto his back, and he flew, spreading his wings and circling upward, higher and higher. At last, he was so exhausted he could go no farther.

(continued on page 105)

raptors in a very clear hierarchy of flight altitudes. One way a healer calls upon the eagles is by blowing a shrill note on the eagle-bone flute.

11 As Native people know, every raptor and songbird has a certain level in the sky to which they can attain and no further. This story teaches the children the various altitudinal limits of the different birds. The great bald eagle is the chief of birds, because he flies the highest and sees the farthest. Recent experiments in animal communication have shown startling evidence that animals "think," but in ways that are different than humans. For one thing, they may be a lot more intuitive, and also more metaphorical. Native Americans have long known what primate intelligence researchers such as Penny Patterson and Sue Savage-Rumbaugh are just discovering—animals have much to tell us.

In a widespread but now mostly forgotten esoteric Native American tradition, the levels of heaven are marked by the width of one's hand when the arm is extended toward the horizon. There are seven "hands," or levels, up to the highest level that the sun and the rainbow can reach. But the moon and the stars can reach the apex, or zenith, in the sky, which is the twelfth level. In some stories, the various "levels of heaven" to which different birds can attain is a way of expressing the idea that some people have a natural ability to transcend to higher levels of vibration (other dimensions of being or levels of reality) than others. As in this story, we all do what we can to help, using our varied abilities. In the apocryphal Book of Enoch, there are seven levels of heaven and different sets of angels on each level. The Qur'an speaks of seven heavens, as do the Altaic shamans in Siberia and the pre-Islamic Persians. It is also mentioned in the Testament of the Twelve Patriarchs.

The eagle is king of birds because he flies the highest and so outranks other birds. This is a mark of his spiritual power, which is recognized in Europe, China, and India, as well. In Europe, there is a story in which the wren stows away on the head of the eagle. When the eagle reaches as high as he can fly, the wren jumps off and ascends the rest of the way and is therefore known as the "king of the birds" in Europe.

Spider Woman then called on Cooper's Hawk, who came at once, flying wing tip to wing tip with Spotted Eagle. Mole Man and Son of Light (who still had Spider Woman in his right ear) walked over the wings and onto the hawk's back. The hawk carried them higher and higher, but after a while, his strength gave out too. "This is as high as I can go," he said.[11]

Spider Woman called for Gray Hawk to take over. Again Son of Light, Mole Man, and Spider Woman changed birds, and Gray Hawk flew higher than the others. Still, it was not high enough and the three friends transferred to the back of Red Hawk, best of all fliers.

(continued on page 107)

But remember that in Native American stories, every animal has a dark side as well as a light side, and every hero has an anti-hero. So as we work in higher realms of consciousness and power, we must constantly be ready to face greater and greater adversaries. In this story, we get a rare glimpse of the eagle's potential dark side; he misuses his supreme power over all other animals, including humans, and therefore becomes quite scary. Luckily, we have Son of Light, who represents the highest and most spiritual in man, but who needs a great challenge in order to become stronger spiritually. In fact, Son of Light and Man-Eagle will help transform one another into a more balanced male figure, one that can sustain a complete relationship with a woman: a "man for all seasons."

12 The quest for the "top of the mountain" is a universal metaphor for striving for excellence; in a Native American context it has special significance, because the mountain is said to extend to at least the seventh level in the sky. All mountains, when climbed, bring us into the realm of eternal and supernatural beings, whether visible to us or not.

13 Note the hero did not say, "Hey, no problem! I can handle this!" In Native American stories, it is the smart human who humbles himself to ask such questions. Only an idiot would presume to know more than a supernatural being. If we want to be successful, we should pray often and continue to ask questions and for help but be ready to actually hear the answer and accept the help when it comes. This hero is a good example of the "Tool of the Creator," or, as they say in the West, "the Co-worker with God." He proceeds into danger, filled with trust, and sharing the burden of the quest with supernatural guides. There is a widely known expression found in many Algonkian languages, "*Tchee tchan kwee wee,*" which means "Spirit watch over me!" It means that we are surrendering to Spirit, totally. The hero (unlike a lot of young listeners) did not use his mind to try to figure out what Spider Woman would do with the imitation shirt of flint, he just trusted in the process. The children cry out, "What is she going to do with the shirt?" The storyteller says, "Listen and find out! Son of Light had to wait, and so can you!"

Red Hawk flew through a hole (*büchi,* or doorway) in the clouds, right to the white house that was the home of Kwa'toko, Man-Eagle. Thanking Red Hawk for carrying them so far, Son of Light, Spider Woman, and Mole Man got down and walked boldly up to the white house in the clouds.[12]

"Look at the ladder to the entrance," said Spider Woman to Son of Light. "Its rungs are sharp knives, made of shining obsidian. They'll cut your fingers off if you try to get up there."

"What shall we do?" asked Son of Light.[13]

"Go pick some sumac berries," Spider Woman said. Son of Light did not ask why, but went and gathered the berries, and then returned to the same place. "Now feed them to Horned Toad over there," she said.

Again, not doubting her words, Son of Light popped the berries into the wide mouth of Horned Toad, who chewed them into a gooey paste that he then spit into the palm of Son of Light's hand. Rather than wipe it off, he waited for the words of Spider Woman to tell him what to do.

(continued on page 109)

14 There is a positive universal relationship between spiritual need and the witnessing of miracles. If you want to see miracles happen, place yourself in a situation where God will benefit from the miracle, and it will happen. God answers us in wondrous signs, which the Lenape call *keegaynolaywoagun* (*kee-**gay**-no-lay-**woa**-gun*), "the universe is showing (teaching) you something wonderful." To sit around in luxury, serving no great effort or spiritual cause, and then ask to see a miracle is a vain act. It won't happen. Herod asked Jesus to perform miracles for him in his pleasure palace but was not sincere in his desire to know God, although his wife had already seen signs in dreams and warned her husband to be careful.

Place yourself in harm's way to rescue a loved one, and strange things will happen to help you on your way. This scene in the story is just one of many such miracles.

The transformation of sumac berries into paste and sharp knives into blunt stones is as symbolic as it is miraculous. The sumac berries are poison, and the horned toad is an ugly-looking creature; both represent fear. His name is *pachipkwasha* (***patch**-ip-**kwa**-sha*), literally "gown of buffalo skin." The obsidian is a volcanic stone, forged by fire into a glasslike rock that is indeed sharp. I believe on one level it represents the cutting words that a father sometimes says to a son, which "cut off our fingers," a terrible form of punishment from time immemorial. Son of Light must overcome his fear of punishment in order to proceed further. On a literal level of meaning, the sumac berries dull the taste. The original narrator cited the well-known effect of sour berries taking the edge off the teeth. In fact, vinegar, a related substance, dissolves granite, just as water dissolves limestone and wind dissolves sandstone. So the story may be factually true.

15 A *viga* is the trunk of a tree, typically pine or spruce, that has been peeled and used as a rafter or roof support column.

16 The wife does not possess the frame of mind to trust in Spirit and doubts even as she is being rescued. This is reminiscent of the Buddhist stories of the bodhisattvas who go through great trouble to "res-

"Now smear what Horned Toad has given you onto the sharp edges of the rungs," Spider Woman told him. As Son of Light smeared the edges, they immediately became blunt so that he could climb up without having his fingers cut off.[14]

Spider Woman was still in his right ear, while little Mole Man had buried himself in Son of Light's hair. With his two hidden companions, Son of Light stepped into Man-Eagle's white house.

The first thing he saw was Man-Eagle's magic shirt of flint, made from a hundred arrowheads, hanging from a *viga*.[15] Quick as a flash, Son of Light hung the counterfeit shirt on that rafter and put the real shirt on. They were so alike that not even Son of Light could tell them apart. He went into the second room and found his wife, her hands tied behind her back.

"I've come to free you!" he told her.

(continued on page 111)

cue" a disdainful humanity from spiritual ignorance. The teaching in both cases is that the spiritual hero is detached from the fruits of his labors; although he extends his hand to assist all who are trapped in illusion, he knows that many will refuse help, and that is their right.

17 Some would see this as a reference to the teaching that we live on after death and go to a happier place.

18 Smoking the pipe is a manly art, although in many tribes, women are permitted to smoke. Man-Eagle has plenty of male power and sees that Son of Light is weak in this area. The poison pipe contest also is found in the Navajo story of the warrior twins seeking to atone with their father. In that story, the poison pipe is a test to see if they are truly the sons of the Sun, and immortal. Glooskap, the Mi'kmaq folk hero, was famous for his pipe smoking, and was approached by an evil and murderous *m'teoulin* (*m'teou-lin*), or magician, who sat down in front of Glooskap with a very long pipe, which had an extremely large bowl, and began to smoke it, burning it all in one long breath. Then he blew all the smoke at Glooskap, tauntingly, also in one breath. Glooskap pulled out his pipe and as he put it in his mouth, the bowl grew ten times its size. He, too, burned all the tobacco in one breath, but when he blew the smoke back at his rival, the ground split open. Glooskap said, "There. If you can do that, you may kill me." The man could not and walked away in defeat.

"Flee!" she cried. "Run quickly! No one who enters here ever leaves alive!"[16]

"Don't be afraid," he answered gently, untying her hands. "We'll all come out of here alive and happy!"[17]

Man-Eagle was asleep in the next room, but Spider Woman was carrying a "hear-nothing" charm that prevented their noise from reaching his ears. Unaware that strangers were in his house, he awoke and put on his shirt of flint (the imitation one made of piñon), then went into the next room. "Now I will enjoy the beautiful girl! Ha ha ha!" he thought, but, instead, found himself face-to-face with Son of Light. "Who are you?" asked Man-Eagle. "How dare you come in here!"

"You have stolen my wife, and I am taking her back now."

"Maybe you will, and maybe you won't," said Man-Eagle. "You are a big talker, but instead of war between us, let us gamble to decide that, and you must abide by the consequences. If you lose, I shall slay you." To this the youth agreed.

"You and I will engage in a contest," said Man-Eagle.

"What kind of contest?" inquired Son of Light.

"A smoking contest!" gloated Man-Eagle.

The monster brought out a huge pipe, as long as a large-sized man, and filled it with tobacco. "We will both smoke this," he told Son of Light, "and whoever weakens and faints is the loser. If you lose, I have the right to kill you and then have my way with your lovely wife. If you win, you can take her back."

Now, Man-Eagle's magic tobacco was poisonous enough to stun anyone who was not used to it, though it no longer had an effect on him.[18] But while Man-Eagle explained the rules of the contest, Mole Man quickly burrowed a hole in the floor underneath the spot on which Son of Light was sitting. Mole Man made a passage all the way

(continued on page 113)

19 Son of Light, in other words, becomes the sacred pipe. As the good smoke is prayer, we ourselves can become the hollow vessel for spirit, and by not holding onto the experience, we will not experience any negative energy that is sent our way. This teaching is somewhat parallel to St. Francis of Assisi saying, "Let me be an instrument of thy peace," or Jalaluddin Rumi proclaiming himself the *Masnavi*, "the reed of God." It means "getting out of our own way," as Alan Watts often said. Another teacher, John Roger, used to say that "Get the hell out of my way" was a lot like saying "Get Heaven in my way," but we just don't realize it.

20 In another version, the antlers are not switched, but Son of Light insists on choosing first, and chooses the ones Spider Woman tells him to. Like the stag in the *Mabinogion*, the elk's horns are also seasonal. The ability of Man-Eagle to change with the seasons gives him his stability and his mortality. Elk medicine is sexual medicine, but usually saved for rare moments. The most dramatic aspect of that kind of sexuality is the competition between male elks as they rut and bash their large elk horns against each other to see who will be the alpha male. This scene is therefore a much-transmuted contest of sexual prowess. Mother Nature (Spider Woman) plays a trick on Man-Eagle. He becomes sexually "fragile," while Son of Light is "hard as stone."

down through the earth to the outside, and as the man and monster puffed away, the smoke passed right through Son of Light, through the hole and down, and then into the outside air. The two smoked and smoked until Man-Eagle got dizzy from his own magic tobacco and had to stop. Son of Light, on the other hand, was unaffected.[19]

Filled to the bursting point with smoke, Man-Eagle stepped outside the house to clear his head. Son of Light followed, and they both saw dense clouds of smoke covering the sky. "I wonder how he did it," thought Man-Eagle. "And where did all those clouds come from?" Then he said, "Well, you win this contest, but this is only the first one. Now comes the second test."

Man-Eagle brought two large elk antlers into the room. "Take this one," he told Son of Light, "and I'll take the other. Each of us will try and break his own in two. If you fail to break yours with your hands, I shall kill you and take your wife for my evil pleasure!"

Well, Son of Light had to try to stop him. The antler that Man-Eagle had given his rival was actually a magical piece of stone—in fact, the hardest stone in the world. The antler that Man-Eagle kept for himself was a false one made of a brittle wood called *chim'ona*. Quick as a flash, just before the contest began, Spider Woman, who, possessing all the powers of the earth and sky, and who could not only change size like the shadows but could move with blinding speed like lightning, exchanged the two elk antlers. She did the switch with such speed that not even the eagle eyes of the great monster could follow her. Son of Light broke his antlers easily, but Man-Eagle could not break his, no matter how hard he tried. "I wonder how he *did* that!" thought the monster. He was not so sure of himself anymore.[20]

"Well, well, this was just child's play, something to warm us up," said Man-Eagle. "Now for the third contest."

(continued on page 115)

21 Roots have to do with grounding and centering. One must have deep-rooted strength if he is to uproot a tree.

"What is it this time?" asked Son of Light.

"Step outside with me," said Man-Eagle. They went out, and the monster pointed to two huge pine trees near his white house. "You choose one of those trees and I will choose the other, and he who fails to pull his tree up by the roots loses the contest. If I win, I'll kill you and possess your wife."

"So be it," answered Son of Light, wondering if his friends Spider Woman and Mole Man were going to be able to get him out of this one.

Man-Eagle chose the tree that he thought had shallower roots. "Remember," he said, "if you fail to pull up your tree—trunk, branches, root and all—you lose, no matter what I do."[21]

During these preparations, Mole Man had burrowed underneath Son of Light's tree and gnawed through all the roots. Son of Light therefore was able to pull up the tree easily, while Man-Eagle could not uproot his own. Son of Light threw his tree over a cliff. "It pleased me to let you win once more," Man-Eagle told Son of Light, "but you must win the fourth and last contest." But to himself, he said, "I *wish* I knew how he did that! This young man must be strong indeed!"

"What do you propose?" asked Son of Light.

"An eating contest! Watch me," answered Man-Eagle. He began carrying into his biggest room heaps of food: meat of all kinds, piki bread and corn bread of all kinds, mush and gruel of all kinds, squash and bean dishes of all kinds, meats, stews, and porridge, baskets full of wafer breads, pots, cups, and dippers full of food. Making two mountains of it all, he told Son of Light, "This is your heap and that one over there is mine. You must eat your heap all at once, without leaving a scrap. If you can't do it, I will kill you and then take your wife.

(continued on page 117)

22 │ An eating contest is a classic American experience, one of the most basic contests of all, and has Native American roots. In Native circles, being a big eater is still considered the sign of a strong, hardworking man. It is a sign of great health and vitality. Son of Light is not nearly as big or strong as Man-Eagle, so he has to use a "hollow leg" to win, which he does. The somewhat scatological implications are meant to add a touch of humor to the tale.

23 │ Vulnerability is one of the gifts of Son of Light, but he must learn from Man-Eagle how to also be invulnerable in order to be chief.

24 │ Although obviously strong and powerful, we can guess that Man-Eagle isn't really that smart. Spider Woman apparently knew this and found a way to outsmart him at every turn. She had the resin shirt made knowing that eventually the monster would be tempted to exploit the fireproof qualities of flint, which is also associated with making fire (hence "firestone"). As mentioned, the early heroes used magic and cunning to outwit evil, all without conventional violence. It makes for a much better story. There are many layers of meaning to Man-Eagle's transformation by fire: he finally experiences passion; he finally puts aside his stony exterior; he finally gives himself over to Spirit; he becomes humbled, or he lights the Bel fires of spring, which encourages the sun to enter into its full mature power.

"I'm sure to win this one," Man-Eagle said to himself. "This young man is puny compared to me; he can't possibly absorb all this food!"

Again, Mole Man dug a tunnel underneath Son of Light. As quickly as Son of Light emptied a dish, the food passed through him and through the tunnel to a large pit someplace outside the house. In no time, Son of Light had eaten the whole mountain of meat, corn, squash, beans, piki, and mush. Man-Eagle tried to match him dish for dish, but could not.[22]

"Well," said Son of Light, "I guess I'll take my wife back now and go home!"

"Not so fast!" said Man-Eagle. "In the end it comes down to strength and endurance: Which of us is invulnerable? Which of us can withstand the flames of a great fire? I can. Can you? We shall see!"[23]

Man-Eagle created two large piles of dry wood. "You stand on this one, I'll stand on that one. Your wife can set fire to them once we are in position. If you can withstand this fire, then I'll do whatever you say."

He thought to himself, "Ha ha! Now I can get rid of this upstart. My magic shirt of flint is fireproof, but this young dog will be burnt up. I will win easily." This was just the test that Spider Woman had foreseen and had prepared for.

Son of Light's wife nervously set fire to the two woodpiles, lighting each in the northwest, southwest, northeast, and southeast. Of course, Son of Light was wearing the real magic shirt of flint, made from a hundred arrowheads. Now coated with ice by the power of Spider Woman's magic, it protected him from the flames. The ice melted and the drops extinguished the fire. But the shirt that Man-Eagle wore was made of resin, one of the most flammable materials in nature. It ignited in such a flash that, within seconds, only ashes remained of the once-great monster.[24]

(continued on page 119)

25 The resurrection from the ashes is an ancient metaphor for spring and for the regeneration of the spirit. It is said among the Ojibway that ashes can absorb any kind of bad energy, or witches' spells, and counteract them. Here, the ashes undo the bad magic of Man-Eagle in a very direct way. However, there is another level of meaning to this story when we see this character as a dark side of Thunderbird. In Algonquin stories of Quebec, there is a good man who is killed by jealous men, then cut up, and then burned. Three days later, a glorious Thunderbird arises from the ashes and flies away. This story is exactly the reverse: the jealous bird is killed and burned to ashes and arises again as a good man. Perhaps some day this same good man will again be burned and will rise up as a Thunderbird, completing a great cycle of transformation and rebirth, similar to the phoenix stories of China and Persia.

26 Son of Light—with help from Spider Woman—did not actually kill Man-Eagle; he transformed him from an evil spirit into a good man, in a sense a sort of exorcism of the universe. Spider Woman knew that Man-Eagle had to reach his *katabasis,* a Greek word meaning "inner death." In other words, he had to give up the ego, dive down into the pit of ashes, and hit bottom before he could be reborn in the flesh. She had the medicine all prepared, and knew all along how he would die and be reborn a new man. She is very old and has seen many kings come and go.

In the Native American hero concept, the warrior does not win by destroying the enemy, but wins by transforming the enemy into a friend. To do this, he must get close to the enemy, or the one who thinks himself the enemy, and this takes skill, cunning, and fearlessness. In the Way of the Heron, the peacemaker's path of the Algonquin people, which is the true Way of the Hero as well, it takes skill and daring and bravery to open lines of communication with the enemy long enough to make a friend out of him. The Mi'kmaq pipe carriers say, "*Madenaq gehweenoo delliah delawen,*" "I am a warrior of the truth."

Then Spider Woman whispered into Son of Light's right ear. "Take this marvelous medicine of mine in your mouth and then spurt it all over Man-Eagle's ashes."

Without doubting, and without arguing or questioning what he was told, Son of Light did what Spider Woman asked, and he spat the medicine over the ashes. A great being arose from the ashes, now transformed into a good-looking and kind man.[25] He was no longer an eagle.[26]

Spider Woman addressed Eagle-Turned-Into-a-Man. "Have you learned your lesson? Will you stop killing and eating people? Will you stop stealing and abusing wives and maidens? Will you promise?"

(continued on page 121)

In the end, it turns out that these large forces of nature and of fate were using Son of Light to help Man-Eagle reach a turning point in his life where he would become enlightened to his own true nature.

27 Man-Eagle will do it again, no matter what he promises, because of the cycle of eternal return. Until the two men learn from each other and become as one, Man-Eagle will continue to banish the sun god in November and hold the Goddess of the Land in his dark clutches until May.

28 As this symbolically retells the story of May, the sun reclaims the earth, and the corn stalks and other plants stand up again like people who have been brought back to life. In another version, the victims have not been killed but only held captive and are freed by Son of Light. Son of Light does not necessarily foresee this glorious outcome— he is but a humble tool of the Creator. In any case, it is a happy ending worthy of the hero's struggle.

Eagle-Turned-Into-a-Man said, "I promise I will never do evil again! *Anchai!* Yes!"[27]

Son of Light joyfully reclaimed his wife, while Spider Woman brought all the Hopi people whom Man-Eagle had killed back to life again.[28] Then they all climbed onto the backs of Eagle, Hawk, Gray Hawk, and Red Hawk, and these good birds carried them safely back home.

1 Much of mythology and religion has its birth in the early roots of various world cultures, and the balance between water and land is of great importance to all indigenous people. So just as almost every culture has a "flood story," almost every culture has a "drought story" as well, and a hero for both occasions.

☐ Agulabemu, the Great Bullfrog (Mi'kmaq)

In the old times, there was a Mi'kmaq village far away among the mountains and little known to other men. The people were very happy, with good feelings. The men hunted deer every day, the women did the work at home, and all went well. The village was next to a brook. Besides the brook, there was not a drop of water in the land except in a few rain puddles. No one there had even found a spring.

Now the people liked good water. The brook was very good, and they became very fond of it. But after a time they noticed that the brook was beginning to run low, and not just in the summer, but in the autumn too, even after a rainfall. Day by day it diminished, until its bed was as dry as a bone in the ashes of a dead fire.[1]

Now it was said that far away upstream, where none had ever been, there was another village, but what sort of people lived there, no one knew. And thinking that these people of the upper country might be in some way involved in the drought, they sent a messenger to investigate the matter.

After he had traveled three days, he came to that village, and found that a dam had been raised across the stream so that no water could pass. All the water was kept in a pond. He asked them why they had done this, since the dam was of no use to them. They told him to go and see their chief by whose order the dam had been made.

When he came to the chief, there sitting lazily in the mud was a creature more like a whale than a man, though he had a human form. For he was immense to measure, like a giant—fat, bloated, and brutal

(continued on page 125)

2 | In the Chinese tale of the four water dragons, we can find many striking similarities to the Agulabemu story. There were no rivers or lakes on earth, only the Eastern Sea, in which lived four dragons. Once, while they were playing together in the clouds, the Pearl Dragon looked down at humankind and saw that the people were praying for rain, but there was none. The earth was cracked and parched and the people were dying. The Long Dragon said, "Let's go and beg the Jade Emperor for rain!"

Jade is a very hard stone, and he was a very hard emperor, and he said, "You should have stayed in the sea and minded your own business, but never mind. Go home, and I will send some rain tomorrow!"

The dragons went back to the sea, but it did not rain. The four dragons wept because they knew the Jade Emperor only cared about his own pleasure and never took the people to heart.

The Long Dragon said, "Look, there is plenty of water in the sea. We'll dive down and scoop it up in our mouths and spray it toward the sky. The water will come down as rain and save the people."

"Good idea," said the Black Dragon. "But the Jade Emperor will be very angry when he hears of this. He might kill us."

The Yellow Dragon said, "I will do anything to save the people. We will never regret it if we try." Soon the clouds were dark with rain.

The God of the Sea discovered these events and reported back to the Jade Emperor. The emperor was enraged and sent four mountains to lay upon the dragons so they couldn't escape. The mountains flew through the air and landed on the dragons. Still determined to do good for the people, they turned themselves into four rivers: the Heilongjian (Black River), the Huanghe (Yellow River), the Changjiang (Yangtze or Long River), and the Zhujiang (Pearl River).

The parallels between the two stories, the two villains, and the two heroes are striking. Agulabemu is the Jade Emperor of the story, and Glooskap is the dragon. It is only in Middle Eastern, Indic, and European cultures that the dragon is evil. In Chinese culture it represents masculine powers of water and rain, like the nagas (serpent-beings)

to behold. His great yellow eyes stuck from his head like pine knots, his mouth went almost from ear to ear, and he had broad, skinny feet with long toes that were amazing! The messenger complained to this monster, "I am thirsty! *Gehdoo samqwai!* I am dry! *Geespasee!*" The monster first said nothing, and then croaked, and finally replied in a loud bellow:

"Do as you choose, do as you choose, do as you choose."

"What do I care? What do I care? What do I care?"

"If you want water, if you want water, if you want water, go somewhere else!"

Then the messenger described the suffering of the people, who were dying of thirst, and this seemed to please the monster, who grinned. At last he got up and, making a single leap to the dam, took an arrow and bored a hole in it, so that a little water trickled out, and then he bellowed, "Up and be gone, up and be gone, up and be gone! *Skootamundjai* (**Skoot**-*a*-*mun*-**djai**)!"[2]

(continued on page 127)

of India. This reversal of symbols allows the frog to be both a European dragon figure and a Chinese emperor at the same time.

In Chinese lore there is a connection between dragons and royalty, which gives us insight into the meaning of the frog king of the Wabanaki (Algonquins of the Northeast), as both animals are amphibians. Each has a tendency to "suck up" all the life-giving resources, leaving the common people to starve, as occurred in Russia under the tsars. Each of these stories makes it clear that power is not to be trusted, which is one of the most consistent themes in Native American stories.

3 One remarkable thing about Glooskap is the extensive parallels that exist between him and Indra, the great cultural hero of India and father of Arjuna. One might suspect the Mi'kmaq of borrowing, but the Mi'kmaq are descendants of a people who have lived in the same place for over 10,000 years, and Indra comes to us from the Vedas, which were first sung not earlier than 1500 B.C.E. The Vedas describe Indra as "he who gave birth to the sun and the dawn and led out the waters, he my people, is Indra." Glooskap is the father of the People of the Dawn, the Wabanaki; some say he arrived from the east at dawn, some say he was created out of the clay on the eastern shore when hit by a lightning bolt. He is associated with water and the rainbow. Indra brought water to the earth and his bow is a rainbow. Indra rides a steed that is "swift as the wind," and Glooskap runs through the forest "swift as the wind."

4 Indra is the god of war and weather and loves a good fight and the heroism of men. Glooskap, who loves heroism as well, has mastery of the Wind Eagle, Wuchosen, who controls the weather.

5 In art, Indra is always depicted as a muscular red man with four arms, one for each of the four directions. We don't know if Indra's feathers were red and black as were Glooskap's feathers, but in Lenape (a people related to Mi'kmaq) lore, red represents the red light of morning, and black the color of the night sky; together they represent the polarities of the world brought into balance and the acceptance of things as they are.

So the man left, little comforted. He came to his home, and for a few days there was a little water in the stream; but this soon stopped, and there was great suffering again.

Now these people, who were the most honest people in the world and never did harm to anyone except their enemies, were in a bad way. For it is a bad thing to have nothing but water to drink, but to lack that as well is to be mightily dry. And Glooskap, who knew all that was passing in the heart of humans, took note of this, and when he willed it, he was among them, for he always came as the wind comes, and no one knew how.[3]

Just before he came, all of these people had decided in council that they would send the bravest man among them to almost certain death. He would go to the village that had built the dam. Either he would break the dam or do something desperate. He would go armed and sing his death song as he went.

Then Glooskap, who was very pleased with all this, as he loved a brave deed, came among them looking terribly ferocious.[4] In the land there was not one who seemed half so frightening. For he appeared ten feet high, with a hundred red and black feathers in his hair. His face was painted like fresh blood[5] with green rings around his eyes and a large clam shell hanging from each ear. A spread eagle, very awful to behold, flapped its wings while standing on his right shoulder, so that as he walked into the village, all hearts quaked. Needless to say, they admired him greatly. Then Glooskap, having

(continued on page 129)

6 Indra battles a huge serpent named *Vritra,* which means "the Encloser" (or "the Swallower"), who is the size of the largest mountain (or, in some versions, who lives on a mountain). Glooskap battles a huge amphibian named Agulabemu who lives on a large mountain. His name means "without understanding of truth," and implies he is greedy. Vritra's eyes blaze like the sun. As a bullfrog, Agulabemu's eyes are also large, "bigger than his stomach," also blazing like the sun.

7 Dirty water is an idiomatic expression in Mi'kmaq that means "bad medicine," a possible reference to black magic. I have heard *metcheegeb-wag (**met**-tchee-ge-**bwag;** "dirty water") or wedjiwintchik (**we**-dji-**win**-tchik)* used to refer to bad medicine. On several levels, Agulabemu was playing a trick on him.

8 The huge monster Vritra, an *asura* (power-hungry being), stole all the water in the world, "holding the waters of heaven captive in its belly." Agulabemu (who is also obviously power hungry) stole all the water in the world and held it captive in his belly. Indra had to pass through Vritra's ninety-nine fortresses, and then he killed the monster Vritra, piercing his belly with a thunderbolt, releasing the water "to circulate once more through the body of the world." Glooskap had to go through various stages of the mountain to get to Agulabemu and open his belly with a spear, releasing water back into the world. However he does not kill him, as that kind of hero represents a later stage of "civilization," or a downward transformation, as Joseph Campbell would put it.

In another version of the Indra tale, Vritra opens his huge mouth and swallows Indra whole. Indra does not die but pulls out a special knife made from the backbone of a holy man and opens Vritra's abdomen, emerging whole and unharmed, which parallels Glooskap's spear opening Agulabemu's belly. Of course, Jonah and the whale come to mind. Jonah prayed to God to release him from the belly of the great fish, and he was vomited out.

9 The squeezing of the frog in Glooskap's hand is not only unique in mythology, but quite clever, turning it into a "Why?" story for children, who can then examine the back of any frog and see where Glooskap's fingers were.

heard the whole story, told them to cheer up. He would soon make everything right.[6] He went up the bed of the brook, and, coming to the town, sat down and said to a young man, "Bring me water to drink." The boy said that no water could be had in that town unless it was given out by the chief. "Go then to your chief," said the master, "and bid him hurry, or I will know the reason why." And this being told, Glooskap received no reply for a long time, and sat on a log smoking his pipe. Then the boy returned with a small cup, barely half full of very dirty water.[7]

So he stood up and said to the boy, "I will go and see your chief, and I think he will soon give me better water than this." And having come to the monster, he said, "Give me water to drink, and the best, at once, you Thing of Mud!" But the chief said, "Get out of here. Go find water where you can." Then Glooskap thrust a spear into his belly, and there gushed forth a mighty river, even all the water that should have run before, for he had put it into himself.[8] And Glooskap, rising high as a giant pine, caught the chief in his hand and crumpled his back with a mighty grip. And it was Bullfrog. So Glooskap threw him with contempt into the stream, to follow the current. And ever since that time, the bullfrog's back has wrinkles in the lower part, showing the prints of Glooskap's awful squeeze.[9]

Then he returned to the village; but there he found no people— not one—for an amazing thing had occurred during his absence. These villagers had said, "Suppose you had all the nice, cold, fresh, sparkling, delicious water there is in the world? What would you do?"

One said that he would live in the soft mud, and always be wet and cool.

(continued on page 131)

10 Diti was another enemy of Indra, whose children Indra had killed. Diti then kept a monster child in her womb for a century, training him magically to kill Indra. When Indra found out, he threw a thunderbolt at Diti's belly and shattered the monster into the Maruts, a group of less-powerful storm gods. This is reminiscent of Glooskap throwing a spear at the frog's belly, giving rise to the various forms of sea life.

11 Not surprisingly, there are biblical and Talmudic parallels as well. The second of the ten plagues in Exodus was of frogs, and it was apparently one of the more intolerable curses, as Pharaoh begged Moses to make them disappear. They died instead, making a terrible stench. Agulabemu is clearly a caricature of a bad chief who wants to be like a pharaoh. It is written in a Midrash that "at first only *one* frog emerged from the River, but as the Egyptians struck it, it split into swarms and swarms of frogs, which inundated the land." Again we are reminded of the way that all sea life took form after Agulabemu was struck down by Glooskap, which is a blessing for all who survive on seafood, and is the opposite of the curse Pharaoh brought upon his people by acting cruelly. As they say, what goes around comes around.

Another said that he would plunge from the rocks and take headers, diving into the deep, cold water, drinking as he dived. And the third, that he would be washed up and down with the rippling waves, living on the land, yet always in the water. Then the fourth said, "You don't know how to wish, but I will teach you. I would live in the water all the time, and swim around in it forever."

Now it turned out that these things were said in the hour that when it passed over the world, all the wishes uttered by people are granted. And so it was with these people. The first became a leech, the second a spotted frog, the third a crab, which is washed up and down with the tide, and the fourth, a fish. Before this there had been no water-dwelling creatures, and now there were all kinds.[10] The river came rushing and roaring on, and they all went headlong down to the sea to be washed into many lands all over the world.[11]

7
The Return
of the Sun

[1] Although there is a prevalent association between sun, light, and Creator, this does not mean darkness and night are bad; they are just a different side of the Great Mystery. If the sun was shining all the time, how would the bears feel about it? What would the owls do?

[2] There are two ways to look at this statement: one is to say that there are always those who run from the spiritual, who would rather do anything than look at themselves in the light of day; the other is to say that what is good for one person is bad for another, and vice versa. We tend to forget that not everyone has the same needs we do.

[3] There are other Iroquois stories about the edge of the world in which it is explained more clearly. Storytellers sometimes describe the horizon fancifully as an edge of the sky that tucks in under the edge of the earth, and that two young men who once walked too far west got stuck underneath the edge and couldn't get out.

[4] Each animal has its own survival strategy, a lesson that we do well to learn. The chipmunk always has an exit strategy, a back door through which he or she can escape.

☐ Chipmunk Asks for the Light
(Seneca)

Once long ago, the animals got together to decide whether the world should be forever dark or whether there should be daylight. "Let us have darkness," roared Bear. Chipmunk wanted daylight, and sang, "Light! Light! Let us have light!"[1]

"Night is best," retorted Bear. But Chipmunk chanted over and over, "Let the light come! Let the light come!" and then, as the sky showed its first surprising red dawn in the east, "The light is coming!" Some of the animals ran into the woods to hide and even now only come out at night.[2]

Soon the fire of the sun's rim was brilliant at the edge of the world,[3] and Chipmunk rejoiced. Then the sun rose and daylight filled the sky. Bear was furious and grabbed for Chipmunk with her big paw. Chipmunk did get away into a hole in a log, but not before Bear's claws scratched off some fur, making the stripes on its back that we see today.[4] And even now, every spring, Chipmunk scurries around the woods happily, chattering, "Chip, chip, chip, the light is here!"

1 Many Native stories reveal tribal memories of Paleolithic events. These tales are full of large animals: mastodons, giant beavers the size of bears, and birds that sound like pterodactyls. Often, these animals were destroyed or shrunk in size as punishment for wrongdoing. In this case, the mouse makes a deliberate sacrifice. Either the Natives found the skeletons of these creatures and made stories about them, or they remember them firsthand. The Algonkian-speaking people have pre-Clovis roots which predate the end of the Ice Age. This story, however, reveals an even longer genetic memory than most; it refers to a time before the invention of fire.

2 Native stories meant for children often have a tiny creature as the hero or heroine. This is to foster good self-esteem among children who cannot compete physically with adults, but whose thoughts and deeds are to be respected.

3 Indian corn did not come to the northern climes until about 1000 c.e., so in the early 1800s when this story was told, it is easy to see how the introduction of corn might be fresh in the memory of the oral tradition. The Lenape say the raven flew from the southwest with a single kernel of corn in his beak. The bird dropped it, where it was found by children, and the adults decided to plant it and see if anything grew. It did, and now it is called corn.

☐ Little Brother Gets Mad at the Sun (Winnebago)

There was a time when a thousand men would not be a match for a mouse, as she used to be in ancient times, in the days of the Great Dormouse, the largest of beasts. In the times of the legends, there were more animals than men and the dormouse was the fiercest of them all.[1] This is a story about a brother and sister and their memorable deeds, but if not for the dormouse, we would not be here to share this story.[2]

In those days, people did not eat the animals. They lived on berries and roots and wild vegetables. The Great Spirit, who made all things on land and in the sky and water, had not yet given men *mondamin (mon-da-min)*, the Indian corn. There was no fire to give them heat or to cook with. In the entire world there was just one small fire, watched by two old witches, who let no one approach it. And, until Coyote stole this fire, what food people could manage to get had to be eaten raw, the way it grew. They were always hungry.[3]

There were so many animals, larger than those of today, and so few men, that the animals ruled the earth. The biggest of them all was *Boshkwadosh (Bosh-kwa-dosh)*, the mastodon. He was taller than the tallest trees, and had a huge appetite. He did not stay long on earth, or there would not have been enough food for the other animals. Boshkwadosh finally disappeared, but by that time there were only two human beings left standing on Mother Earth, a young girl and her little brother.

(continued on page 139)

4 Does the smallness of Little Brother indicate his spiritual stature or an early understanding of the Napoleon complex? Or is it a clue from the oral tradition about what really happened thousands of years ago? On the Indonesian island of Flores, scientists recently found humanoid skeletons from eighteen thousand years ago that are three feet tall full grown, the same size as Little Brother. They are now called *Homo floresiensis,* and they are the "little brothers" of the human race. *Homo floresiensis* used tools and apparently were good sailors.

5 Young boys were often given a toy in the form of a tiny bow and arrow. Girls were often given small dolls to play "mother" with. It seems possible that this story owes some of its inspiration to the presence in the home of such toys, as they would make excellent story-telling aids.

≡ In this story, children are encouraged to see things from the animals' point of view. What if you were in their position, always having to run away from large humans carrying weapons? What would it feel like to have to worry about extinction? This theme greatly distinguishes Native American culture from European. Western culture did develop systems of ethics between humans (or at least certain humans), but nature was not clearly part of the deal. In general, Native American teachings emphasize our ethical obligations to nature and to "wild animals," as well as to each other. In fact, the whole idea of there being something called "animals" separate from humans is absurd from both a scientific and Native American perspective. We are animals too, and yet there is a difference. This story plays with that delicate balance between ourselves as humans and the *other* animals, and the elusive "difference" between us.

6 Of course a snowbird is a tiny thing, and only a tiny arrow, shot by a tiny archer, could hit him. The narrator is placing our focus on the very small, preparing us for a surprise of large proportions.

The boy was a dwarf[4] who never grew to be more than three feet high. Since the sister was larger and stronger, it was she who gathered all the food, and cared for him in every way. Sometimes she would take him along with her when she went out to gather roots and berries and herbs. She was afraid that if she left him alone, a large bird might come and carry him off to its nest.

One day she said, "Look, little brother, I have made you a bow and some arrows. It is time you learned to take care of yourself; so when I am gone, practice shooting, for this is something every man should know how to do.[5]

Winter was coming, and to keep himself from freezing, the boy had only a light robe woven by his sister from the wild grasses. He thought to himself, "How can I get something warmer to wear? I am tired of being cold!"

As he said this, a flock of snowbirds flew down nearby and began pecking at fallen logs to get the worms. He looked at their feathers and said, "Those feathers would make for me a nice warm winter coat!"

He tried to shoot them with his little bow and arrow, but had not yet learned to shoot straight, and was wide of the target. He shot at them a second and then a third time. By then, the birds became scared and flew away.

Each day, he tried again, aiming at trees, stumps, baskets, pots, and so forth. His sister told him to wait until the snowbird was hunting for grubs in a dead tree. He tried it. At last he killed a snowbird, then another and another. When he had killed ten birds, he was very proud of himself and realized he had enough for a coat. He offered them to his sister and asked her to make him a coat out of the skins and the feathers.[6]

(continued on page 141)

7 There are several clues that the story takes place around the time of winter solstice: the presence of snow, the multitude of snowbirds, the fact that he was cold, and the fact that it was important he find a coat.

8 Although the trickster in Native American stories is usually a blue jay, weasel, or coyote, in this case it is the human being. As we have seen, there are many stories around North America where there are twin boys, one evil or a "trickster" and one good. In "Little Brother Gets Mad at the Sun," the girl is good, and though the boy is not necessarily evil, he is a trickster, and does foolish, selfish things. Little Brother is similar to Moongarm, the evil wolf in the story of Ragnarok in the Eddas, who eats the moon during an eclipse. The sun symbolizes God, and the boy our own lesser self, our dark side. For him to get mad at the sun is as foolish as for us to get mad at God for our own misfortunes—and yet we all do sooner or later.

His sister made the coat, and also made soup out of the birds' meat, which must have been a very small bowl of soup! It was the first warm winter coat the boy had ever had. It was very attractive and the feathers helped keep out the winter wind.[7] He strutted up and down in front of the wigwam, like a little turkey cock. "Is it true that you and I are the only people living on earth today?" he said. "Perhaps I will go look around and see if there is anyone else."

Because of his size, his sister feared that harm might come to him, but off he went. He didn't find any people. Since his legs were so short, and he was not used to taking long walks, he soon grew tired. When he came to a bare spot on the edge of a hill where the sun had melted the snow, he lay down and went to sleep.

As he slept, the sun played a terrible trick on him. The bird skins were still fresh and tender, and in the heat of the sun they began to shrink and shrivel. His coat became tighter and tighter. He woke up with a start, suddenly finding it hard to breathe. He got up and looked at what had happened, and angrily tore off his coat, ruining it in the process. The sun was sinking in the west. The boy faced the sun and shook his fist. "See what you have done?" he said with a stamp of his foot. "You have spoiled my new birdskin coat! You think you are all-powerful and out of my reach, but I will get revenge on you for this! Wait and see!"[8]

He went back to his sister and told her what had happened. His sister thought him foolish for wanting revenge on the sun. The boy stretched out on the ground, where he stayed for ten days without eating or moving. Then he turned on his side and lay there for another ten days. Finally, he rose to his feet. "I have made up my mind. I will catch the sun in a noose. Find me some kind of cord, with which to make a snare."

(continued on page 143)

9   Rope making can be easily demonstrated using three or more strands of grass, as an illustration of the tale. It is a useful skill for Native American children to learn.

10   In ancient times, and in shamanistic societies, the sun is a symbol of all that is good, of Creator. It is believed that it is our duty to bring up the sun in the east with our songs and ceremonies. If there is no one to sing up the sun, it will not come up. This is a metaphor for our own importance as co-creators with the universe, our oneness with the ongoing fact of Creation, and the importance of our prayers in the spiritual world. However, here is a situation where, for the first time, no human being is around who will sing up the sun. In fact, this human has done the opposite and has attacked the sun, the principle of goodness, to get revenge. This shows the potential foolishness of future human beings.

Even in ancient times, people would note the place of the rising of the sun in the east by its closeness to a certain hill or rock on the horizon on any given day.

Just to the north of the Winnebago of Lake Superior are the northernmost Cree, who have contact with people even farther north. During the winter, from about December 18 to December 24, at certain latitudes, the sun ceases to come up in the east at all, and there are five days of darkness. It is a yearly spiritual crisis that has given rise to some of the world's greatest spiritual traditions and stories, including this one.

This is the way that the winter solstice looks to the people of the far north. Sometimes, around noon, a glow of light can be seen on the southern horizon, but the complete sun is never visible during those long and frightening days. It is as if the sun were caught in a noose and were struggling to break free of the horizon. The top of his head appears for a few moments, and then he sinks away and all is dark

Sister got some tough grass that grew nearby and twisted it into a rope.[9] She showed it to him. "That's not strong enough. I need a cord that is really strong!" Since he woke from his long sleep he no longer sounded like a boy, but like a man whose words must be heeded.

His sister cut her long, beautiful hair from her head and cut enough to make a cord. When she plaited it, he was very pleased. He took it from her hand and placed it between his lips and it turned to a secret material, and it grew longer and wound around his body.

In the middle of the night he began a long journey toward a certain high hill to the east, and there he fixed the noose at the very place where the sun was going to rise. He hid and waited a long time in the cold and darkness, waiting for the unsuspecting sun to show its face. At last a faint light could be seen in the east. As the sun rose, it was caught in the noose and could not break free no matter how hard it struggled.[10]

When the sun did not rise as usual, the animals were confused and did not know what to do. *Adjidaumo* (A-**djid**-au-mo), Red Squirrel, chattered and scolded from the branch of a tree, to no avail. *Kahgahgee* (**Kab**-gah-gee), Raven, flapped his wings and croaked dire warnings about the coming end of the earth, but to no avail. *Mukwa* (*Muk-**wa***), Bear, did not mind. He had crept into his cave for the winter, and the darker the better as far as he was concerned.

There was no day that day, and no light or warmth at all.

Wabun, East Wind, would usually shoot his silver arrows to chase the darkness from the valleys, but the sun had not yet risen to help him and the arrows fell uselessly to the earth. "Wake up!" Wabun yelled. "Someone has snared the sun! Which of all of you is brave enough to cut the cord?"

Even Coyote, who was the cleverest of all the animals, could not think of a way to rescue the sun. The rays were so hot that Coyote could not get very close to the place where the sun was snared.

(continued on page 145)

again. Incidentally, the animals' names as recorded in this version of the story are not Winnebago, but come from a more northernly latitude—from the Ojibway or Cree.

11 After five days of darkness at the winter solstice, the sun does return. The boy, shortsighted in his anger, did not succeed, and the people are therefore encouraged to resume whatever sun-bringing-up ceremonies they had been taking part in before the unfortunate incident took place.

"Leave it to me!" screamed *Keneu* (*Ken-ay-yoo*), War Eagle. "I often fly close to the sun, and look into the face of the sun without blinking!"

Down he flew toward the sun, and up he came, his feathers singed with fire. Then they woke Dormouse. Once she fell asleep, she usually slept for six months, so it was hard to wake her. Coyote came up close to her ear and howled with all his might, but *Kugebeengwakwa* (literally "Old Blind Woman"), Dormouse, only snored and turned over, almost smashing Coyote flat.

Coyote realized that only the voice of *Annemeekee*, Thunder, could wake Dormouse, so he ran as fast as a coyote can run to its cave in the mountains to seek its help.

Soon Thunder came booming down from the mountain. "Where's Dormouse? I will wake her!" Thunder said. Slowly, Dormouse rose, almost as big as a mountain herself. Thunder kept booming in her ear, making sure she stayed awake, but Dormouse kept closing her eyes again, drifting back toward sleep.

Coyote said, "Dormouse, you are the one who must free the sun. If he burned one of us, we would be just bones. But you are so big, part of you can be burned and there will still be plenty left. As you are the biggest animal, it is expected that you will do the biggest jobs."

Dormouse was not very smart, and was very sleepy anyway, so what Coyote said made a lot of sense, or at least seemed to. She slowly and sleepily made her way to the hill to the east where the foolish little boy had snared the sun, and began to nibble at the noose. As she chewed, her backside got hotter and hotter. Soon it began to burn until the upper part of her body burned away and turned to ashes. At last, she cut through the cord and set the sun free. The sun was very happy and flew up into the sky like an eagle freed from a trap, and the sky became bright again.[11] Dormouse collapsed

(*continued on page 147*)

12 The boy was not so brave as he was stupid, but there are many wryly humorous stories from various nations explaining how we foolish humans got to be "in charge," such as "Why the Blackfeet Never Kill Mice."

on the ground. When the other animals came to find Dormouse, all they found was an animal no larger than an ordinary mouse. She had shriveled up to tiny size, and is still that size today.

Although Dormouse was brave, the foolhardy little brother was braver to have snared the sun, and such was the need for bravery in those days that the animals recognized that humans should be chief over all the animals, at least for a while, and that men should be hunters rather than the hunted.[12]

▤ One remarkable thing about the Raven story is how neatly it dovetails with many of the other stories in this book. The opening scene reminds us of "The Mud Diver Story," with Raven playing the part of Muskrat.

1 If there are no volunteers in a nonmonetary society, the fabric of that society breaks down. There is no light. Here, a fair exchange is offered (the chief's daughter), but when the danger for setting things right is so high, the warrior of truth must care more about intrinsic rewards.

2 This statement is like Chipmunk's "Let there be light!" proclamation. It is also reminiscent of Dormouse in "Little Brother Gets Mad at the Sun."

3 The ridiculing of the newcomer is a classic rite of passage that all would-be heroes of all nations must endure and find a way to cope with. We must have deeper motivations than peer approval. This is why the pipe carrier helps God or Creator serve humanity, but does not serve humanity directly, which would lead to discouragement and, ultimately, corruption.

4 This woman is the dark side of the helpful Grandmother Spider, or Spider Woman. She is the toxic mother, Kali, the dark side of the Great Mother, the Black Darling, Queen of the Underworld, Baba Yaga, the Wild Boar Goddess, and so forth. Robert Bly says the only way for a man to deal with her non-nurturing ways is to stand up to her, like Shiva in the story of Shiva and Kali, and fight back by declaring his boundaries, and that it takes a lot of wildness to do that.

☐ Raven (Tlingit/Salish)

Long ago, there was no light. In one particular village, the people gathered daily to discuss the all-important question of light, and asked volunteers to go out in quest of it. The hand of the chief's daughter was offered as a reward to anyone who was successful in bringing light. There was no lack of volunteers at first, but none of them returned, and soon no one offered himself.[1]

The chief was undaunted and continued calling the meetings and asking for volunteers. One day Raven showed up at a meeting. Raven was sad for the people. He got up and said, "I will bring you light!"[2] This was followed by such loud peals of laughter and mocking hoots that the building almost shook.[3] The chief, who was deep in thought during Raven's harangue, was aroused from his reverie by this sudden outburst of laughter and inquired as to the cause of it. With much derision, the speech and boasts of Raven were repeated to him. Although he had little faith in Raven, the bringing of light was too important to him to let an opportunity slip by.

He congratulated Raven on his noble resolution, encouraged him, and reminded him of the prize that awaited him. Raven, thinking joyfully of his future, flew home to get ready for the trip. He related the story of the day to his grandmother, an old woman. She said, "Better ones than you have tried and failed. How will you, a mere raven, hope to get the light? Why do you want to marry? You smell too strong."[4]

(continued on page 151)

5 Sky Chief is the Sun King, like the solar father of the Hopi and of Son of Light. He is the good side of the Jade Emperor in the Chinese tale of the four water dragons.

6 The pine needle in some versions is a tiny piece of down, in some a speck, in some the leaf of a cedar. It represents the tiny seed of life that is passed between a male and female raven, or a man and a woman, through which we become spirits having a human experience. If Raven's little body and our large bodies both grow from a tiny egg, why couldn't Raven take the form of a human being?

7 This is reminiscent of the white stone canoe of the Ojibway, which represents the shadow soul. The water represents the flow of spirit. When a child is to be born, the spirit goes into the woman's womb like an empty bowl, and takes form. That shape is temporary, like the water in a bowl, when it takes the shape of the bowl. Poured into another vessel, it would take another shape, such as that of a raven.

8 A reference to both the call of the raven, and the "goo goo gaga" of a baby, reminding us that we are not so different from our two-legged relatives, the birds.

Raven was angered and yelled, "You old hag! Who asked you for advice? To spite you, I will marry the Chief's daughter. Even if I'm a raven, I will keep my word to the Chief. And when I return, you do what I tell you, or you will be sorry."

Early the next morning he left the village, and after several days flying in pitch darkness, he saw that the sky was lightening up a bit. He found a light on the horizon. Following the light, he came to a large and cheerful village. The light was so bright it almost blinded him. A strong light was coming from the house of Sky Chief.[5] He perched on a high pine tree and waited and watched. He saw a beautiful young girl emerge from the shining house. She went to the edge of the water, where she knelt and drank some water from a bowl.

Raven changed himself into a pine needle[6] and floated down from the tree, landing on the water. The needle floated unnoticed over to where she was kneeling. When the girl placed her bowl under the water again[7] and lifted it, she snared the floating needle and as she drank, she swallowed it. Nine months later, the girl gave birth to a human child, a small, dark child with small, black, shining eyes and shiny black hair. It was Raven, born as a human boy.

The Sky Chief called him his grandchild and was delighted. He loved him more than he did his daughter. The boy was indulged and humored in all his wishes. He took full advantage and pestered about everything. He handled everything in the house that might have contained light, except three little caskets on a far shelf. He asked to see them, but as the chief was sleeping, no one helped him. He started yelling, "Ga, Ga!"[8] Not wanting to learn the cause of all the disturbance, Sky Chief said, "Oh, give him anything he wants and shut him up!" And he went back to sleep.

(continued on page 153)

9 On two levels, this is a comment on the relativity of what we limit ourselves to think of as "good." Like the dim light in Plato's cave, we look at and are satisfied with a mere glimmer of truth when the brilliant truth of day shines just outside the cave. Raven shows them the pale reflected light of the moon and the distant light of the stars, and to them it seems the greatest of revelations. They are totally satisfied. When he gets the girl, we are satisfied and happy for Raven. In Tlingit society, there are only two clans (or moieties), Raven and Eagle, and Ravens can only marry Eagles. So, although the daughter may literally have been a raven, she still, necessarily, was an Eagle (of the Eagle Clan)!

10 Raven has one more trick to play on us. He reveals to the people a much brighter light, the sun, and while we are laughing at the people in the story for being satisfied with half the light Raven had to offer, Raven laughs at us and ends up with twice as many wives as we would be happy with. He certainly thinks outside the box, that old Raven.

The caskets were handed to the boy and he opened them one by one. In the first was night; the second contained the moon and stars; and in the third was the sun, shining brilliantly. He looked at them for a while, but then shoved them aside, pretending they were worthless to him. A few days later, when no one was around, he turned into Raven again and flew up and grabbed the two boxes full of light and flew away and was never seen by Sky Chief again.

He flew for days. Each day it got darker and darker, until he couldn't see. Finally, he arrived at his own village, reported to the chief, and requested that a meeting be held. When the people were assembled, he said, "I have brought you light!" and reminded them of their promises.

In the presence of all, he opened one of the caskets, and instantly the moon and stars were visible in the sky. The people were all wild with joy, including the chief, who kept his promise and gave his favorite daughter's hand in marriage to Raven.[9]

The next morning Raven called on his new father-in-law, laughing to himself about how easily amused these people were, and asked, "What will you give me if I offer you a still better light, greater than even the moon and stars?"

"My other daughter, I guess," said the stunned chief.

"Call the people, and you shall have the greatest light of all," said Raven.

Raven opened the second box in front of all the people, and instantly it was daylight and the sun shone warmly in the sky. The crowd went wild and Raven bowed his head in dignified acceptance of the crowd's wild adulation, a discrete gesture practiced by every raven and crow since that time.

Since that memorable day the sun, moon, and stars have illuminated the whole world. Raven married the two lovely daughters, with whom he is living very happily to this day.[10]

8
Coyotes and Other Tricksters

1 In some Native American stories, there is no clear boundary between animal beings and human beings. It may be hard to imagine what Deer or Blue Jay looked like standing over a large cooking fire stirring the acorn soup. That's to be expected. We rarely see such animals doing these things. In traditional times, the storyteller would act out the parts of the deer, blue jay, or panther with his or her own human body, using certain gestures, expressions, and movements to make the audience look at the human form and "see" an animal form inside of it. After spending a lot of time around such creatures, it is easier to just "feel" like them, and then the actions are second nature. Native hunters attempt to "become one with" the animal they are hunting and to "think like the fish" they are trying to catch. Storytellers take this one step further.

Each animal tends to do one thing well—a dog rarely makes mistakes at being a dog, and a fox is generally good at being a fox. Humans have the ability to take on the qualities of certain animals at different times. We all have an animal that we remind everyone of, but we can also choose to identify with a different one, and can even take on its survival strategy as our own for a time. We just can't do it as well as they can. We can't always practice being human very well, either. So stories are often told with deliberate ambiguity as to species.

In Native culture, it is considered important to be of a calm, caring and observant state of mind when cooking or preparing food. Deer is the animal most associated with these qualities. Blue Jay is the opposite.

☐ Deer and Blue Jay (Klamath)

On the Klamath River among the Karok Indians, there was a very handsome brave by the name of Panther. All the Indian maidens were in love with him, but he fell in love with Deer and they were married. Deer was very proud to be known as Mrs. Panther and was a splendid wife to him. She was famous for her fine cooking, and all the other women were envious of the tasty acorn soup that Deer cooked.[1]

Blue Jay was also in love with Panther, and although Blue Jay was more beautiful than Deer, she could not cook. She thought, "I'm very beautiful, and if I can just find out how Deer makes acorn soup, maybe I can win Panther away from her.[2] So Blue Jay went to Panther's home and pretended to be a very good friend of Deer's. The second day of her visit at Panther's house, Blue Jay said, "Deer, let me know how you make acorn soup."

"No," said Deer, "you just watch me, and I'll make it alone."

So she took the acorns and pounded them into a very fine flour. Then she sifted and sifted it many times to make it still finer. When the flour was fine as powder she put it in nice clean sand. Then she poured clean, fresh spring water over it all day long. The water kept soaking through the flour down into the sand and took the bitterness out of the acorn flour. When that was finished, she placed her hand in the flour and it stuck on her hand, then she poured fresh water on the bottom of the flour that was on her hand and washed the sand off, and left the flour nice and clean. Then she put the flour in a large cooking basket, added some water to it, and stirred it around with a

(continued on page 159)

2 The idea that Blue Jay thought she could learn to make perfect acorn soup on her first try was proof of her excessive vanity. It also implies a disrespect for Deer, assuming "If Deer can do it, so can I."

3 This story gives us accurate information about how to prepare acorns for mush, soup, bread, or whatever. However, like many Native American stories of the sacred, it can be interpreted on many levels at once. One level of meaning does not preclude the others. It is not just a recipe for acorn soup, but also a recipe for a happy marriage.

Acorns are filled with tannic acid, which is very bitter and poisonous and can even cause vomiting and madness. Brown acorns are much less bitter than green ones, but even brown ones take days to prepare. Making tasty acorn soup is like making fry bread or making love—it takes years to learn to do it right.

4 Bone marrow is more than a flavor, it is considered essential to most Native American diets. I remember as a child having to pick the marrow out of chicken and beef bones and eat the marrow before being free to leave the table. To fail to do this would be terribly wasteful.

5 While Deer has excellent marrow to eat, Blue Jay has hollow wing bones, which do not have any marrow. The idea that Blue Jay's marrow was bitter may be symbolic of the fact that her heart was hollow like her wing bones, and that her love, such as it was, did not remove the bitterness from everyday life for Panther, as Deer's did. In Native American culture, food is life: sweet food, sweet life.

6 The fact that Blue Jay didn't taste the soup first is proof that she didn't really care about Panther as an individual, but was merely trying to impress him, concerned more with appearances and what other people thought. In many stories from various nations, Panther appears as a desirable and sometimes seductive male. As we see in this story, Deer thinks nothing of cracking open her own elbow to make her beloved's food a little tastier. She would break open her own heart for him as well.

wooden paddle. Next Deer took some iron rocks, put them in the fire, and heated them until they were red hot. Then with two sticks she dropped the rocks into the basket of soup, and soon it was boiling.[3]

Then she held her arm over the basket of soup and cracked her elbow open and let some deer marrow pour into the soup. That was her secret of making such tasty soup, by putting the marrow into it.[4] When it had cooked, she served it to Blue Jay and Panther. Both said they had never eaten better soup, and Blue Jay was jealous when she heard Panther praise the acorn soup.

Blue Jay went home, and a few days later she sent for Panther to come to her house for supper. When he arrived, Blue Jay was cooking the acorn soup. She dropped the hot iron into the basket, then cracked her elbow and let the marrow pour into the soup. But instead of making the soup rich and good, her marrow was bitter and spoiled it.[5] Panther tasted the soup and was very angry at Blue Jay for serving him such bitter soup,[6] and he hurried back to his wife, who was still the best cook, according to Panther.

1 This story was probably told originally to Klamath children, and so placing the Klamath in the role of the enemy reminds us that war causes pain and we should be able to place our feet in the enemy's moccasins before we go to attack. In this case, Coyote becomes our ally because we too are Klamath when reading this, and he refuses to fight us. There was no just cause mentioned for the animals and birds to attack.

2 This story is a continuation of the first story in this chapter.

3 Coyote has many different roles; here he is the foolish and greedy comic figure with no common sense, representing the force of human nature.

4 The "Why?" story is a trademark of Native American tales.

5 Wren makes a harsh, insistent call when warning of danger, and apparently sings such a discomforting song just before a storm.

☐ Coyote and Wren (Klamath)

One day Coyote, Wren, and all the little birds and animals went down to the river to fight the Klamath Indians, who lived down the river.[1] Just before they got there, they all stopped to eat. Blue Jay, who had joined the war party, was still trying to learn to cook acorns.[2] While they were cooking, one acorn kept bubbling up in the middle of the pot. Coyote kept watching that acorn and thought it was the only one in the pot. Every time Blue Jay would turn her back, Coyote would try to get the acorn out, but the water was too hot and he could not get it.[3]

After the acorns were cooked, Blue Jay drained the hot water off them, and as the water ran down the hill, lots and lots of acorns rolled out. When the mice saw so many, many acorns, their eyes popped out, and all the mice still have popped eyes today.[4] Coyote ate and ate and ate, but he could not eat all the acorns. And to this day, there are lots of little rocks the shape of acorns where Blue Jay poured the acorns out of the pot.

When the feast was over, Coyote asked Wren to sing a song. Wren said, "My song is very bad, I better not sing."[5]

"Oh, that is all right, go on and sing," said Coyote.

(continued on page 163)

6 | There is a touch of humor in the idea that Wren thinks she causes the storm of which she sings, a reversal of cause and effect. But there may be some truth in her storm predictions, and trickster Coyote may know it. Alfred Lord Tennyson, in *Song of the Wrens*, writes the following verse:

> Gone!
> Gone, till the end of the year,
> Gone, and the light gone with her, and left me in shadow here!
> Gone—flitted away,
> Taken the stars from the night and the sun from the day!
> Gone, and a cloud in my heart, *and a storm in the air!*
> Flown to the east or the west, flitted I know not where!
> Down in the south is a flash and a groan: she is there! she is
> there!

Natives teach much lore about weather signs. Different animals exhibit specific behaviors before a storm or other weather condition.

7 | Many of the oldest stories feature animals and clever heroes who vanquish the enemy or stop a war without violence, just by their wits alone. Here, Coyote is the benevolent "clever hero" who tricks Wren into singing up a storm (which is how much of the wren's musical repertoire is described) in order to prevent a disastrous and unnecessary war. Much of this reminds me of the 1960s in America, where protest singers caused the storm winds of controversy to blow and helped to stop the war in Vietnam. Apparently, it wasn't the first time!

Wren said, "No, my song is too powerful, and it will cause a big storm.[6] I do not want to sing."

But Coyote insisted, so Wren sang. At the very first note of Wren's song, a big windstorm came up, and the first big puff of wind blew Coyote away back up the river, toward his home.

Wren said, "See, I told you my song was very bad."

"That is alright, keep on singing," called Coyote.

Finally, Coyote was blown all the way back home, which was just what he wanted, so he would not have to go to war.[7]

1 Coyote is not always a benevolent trickster. A second type of Coyote story is where he, like Glooskap, is a trickster who learns by doing, and learns by mistakes. The Native American concept of a hero who learns by making mistakes is hard for non-Natives to understand, but it makes sense in teaching tales for children, as we want to encourage them to experiment in order to develop their intelligence, rather than just do what is safe, the tried and true. That is why the little brother who snared the sun is considered a hero, even though he did a foolish thing.

A third type of Coyote story is where he acts on destructive childish impulses so that children can see the terrible results such actions cause. Children learn that not all adults are good, that there are con artists who go through a lot of trouble to fool us. Coyote cons the girls four different times: he pretended to have a salmon, pretended to eat it, pretended to sleep, and then followed them and took their fish. Children need to be wary of strangers, and Coyote is exactly what we should *not* be. He represents powerful, chaotic, and sometimes destructive forces of nature and humanity that we have to deal with but should not imitate. It is important to be cunning when hunting and at war, but we should not be cunning with our friends and family, as Coyote is. In a society that believes in healing by "energy," it is important to maintain the highest ethics to "keep our medicine good." That means keeping our energy strong and free of selfishness, duplicity, and secrecy. Coyote makes us laugh exactly because he acts out our shadow side and tempts us to join him in his folly. In most truly authentic stories, Coyote learns a hard lesson because of his selfish behavior. He heals us through our laughter.

☐ Coyote and the Salmon (Klamath)

Many years ago, there were two Indian girls who lived at the Klamath Reservation on the West Coast of North America. These two girls ate salmon all the time. Now, no one else ever tasted salmon as there were none in the Klamath River, and no one could find out where these girls got their salmon.

One summer, Coyote was very hungry as he was eating just nuts and berries, and he started to think of the two girls and their salmon. The more he thought of it, the hungrier he became. So he went out in the woods and got a large piece of alder bark and cut it in the shape of a salmon. Then he rubbed deer marrow on it for color. He put it in his quiver and started up the river to the girls' house.

The girls had finished eating, but there was a nice fire still burning, so Coyote took out his "salmon," put it on two sticks, and set it up to cook. As it began to cook, the deer marrow dripped off, and the girls wondered where Coyote ever got a salmon, as no one but they knew where to get the salmon.[1]

Coyote took his fake fish, turned his back to the girls, and pretended to eat it. After he had finished he lay down as if to sleep and snored loudly, making the girls think he was asleep.

(continued on page 167)

2 On another level, this story brings us back to a time when the first salmon weir or fish trap was built on the Klamath. Until that time, symbolically speaking, there were no salmon in the river because you couldn't see them. Then when one elder with great cleverness invented the fish trap and placed it in the river, suddenly all these salmon "appeared" out of nowhere, as if by magic, inside the trap. This story captures a moment of realization, the realization of just how many salmon there are in the river. The tale of the "magic" fish trap, like the magic game bag or quiver, is also an old theme that runs through the fireside tales of every nation, just because it makes a good story. It is like the bottomless cup of coffee or the pot that never runs out of porridge. It is a happy thought for hungry children to dream on.

3 The girls only take one salmon at a time. This is a teaching tale about "only taking what you need from nature." A similar lesson is taught in the Glooskap stories of Grandmother Woodchuck's game bag, where Glooskap hunts all the animals at once, to his own disadvantage, and places them all in a single game bag. Here, all the salmon are placed in a single fish trap, which suggests that there are not an unlimited number of salmon "in the world." The fact that all of the world's salmon are in a Klamath family's trap is part of an omphalos tradition in which one's particular tribe is at the center of the world and at the center of Creation. Therefore, the Pandora's box scenario triggered by Coyote's clumsiness and greed is all the more important, as it affects the "whole world." The fact that Coyote was not familiar with the proper methods of handling fish traps is directly caused by the fact that he didn't ask permission and so was not given proper instructions. When we pray to Creator and ask to use "his stuff" (the natural world), it is expected that we too will receive the instructions on how to proceed. If we don't pray, we won't receive the instructions and will do harm to Mother Earth. This is perhaps the oldest teaching of all.

Then the girls built a big fire, so big it burned Coyote's tail, but he stood it and said nothing. The girls decided he was asleep, so they went down to the river, where they had the fish trap—the trap was in the river and had all the salmon in the world in it.[2] The girls raised the top carefully and took out a salmon and went back.[3] When they got back, Coyote was gone.

Coyote had followed the girls, and after they had gone he slipped down and raised the top to get a salmon, but he lifted the top too far and all the salmon jumped out of the trap and swam down the Klamath River. So that is how salmon got in the Klamath River.

9
Nature Spirits, Landkeepers, and Tribal Guardians

1 It is taught among the Washo that the people used to live in harmony with the earth and with each other, and that we can still do that if we live our life in a good way.

The Washo say they were created from the water, whereas the nearby Shoshone say they came from the stars. The Shoshone also see Water Babies but call them by a different name. The Paiute say their whole tribe is descended from Water Babies. The *Me-tsung* (**Mee**-sang) are not subject to human standards of "good" or "bad." They are similar in some respects to the tree spirits of the Lenape, the *Maysingweh*, who are also about sixteen inches high. The word is almost the same.

Nearly every Native American tribe or nation has a body of stories about "little people" but it seems that each language, almost without exception, has a different word for them, which suggests that the idea was not simply borrowed or passed along from nation to nation like so many stories are, but was developed within the tribe.

2 Pine nuts, also called pignolias or *tagum* (**tah**-gum), are still a favorite food of the Washo, as with most Native Americans of the North. The Washo grind them up into a paste or eat them whole. Offerings are a medium of exchange with spirit, and certain foods and plants are considered excellent for offerings, although this varies from tribe to tribe.

3 The Water Babies live in service not to humans, who at best learn by making mistakes, but to those other mysterious forces, which in turn are in service to the Great Mystery. If humans' interests are in conflict with nature's, the Me-tsung will see that nature wins out. In Native American spirituality there is a "way," which some call the Red Road, not unlike the way of the Tao, and it preceded humankind's appearance on earth. What we call "nature" is really not separate from us, but it is larger than the human race, and encompasses us. This nature is not only vast, but it has other interests and priorities that we cannot understand. Nature is not here, as the Bible implies, to serve us, but it will serve us if we first serve it. We are its ward as well as warden, and yet on a deeper level, there is no distinction.

☐ The Meesang, or Water Babies (Washo)

Lake Tahoe is the home of the *Me-tsung* (**Mee**-*sang*), or Water Babies, and in the old times more Washo people could see them because the people were closer to the elements.[1] If they wanted to cross the lake or fish in the lake, they had to prepare by making a basket sealed well with pitch. In it, they put cedar and sage, acorns, bread, and pine nuts.[2] After each basket was full, the owners would put the cover on it and sink it in the lake. By doing this, they believed that the Water Babies would help them to get across safely and give them luck while fishing. But if they didn't bring a basket of food, they believed that the Me-tsung would become very angry. Sometimes people did not return from their trips because they were drowned by the will of the Water Babies.[3]

(continued on page 173)

4 The Washo name for Cave Rock is *De-ek Wadoppush* (*Dee-***eek**-*Wat-tap-***push***), which means Gray Standing Rock. First Light, a Washo elder, explained that in the lowest cave beneath the lake, there is a "spirit lodge" where the spirit of the cannibal "bad Indians"—the *Tanu*—are still being held captive. That is why Washo cannot pass Cave Rock without leaving an offering at that cave to honor them for saving the people, and so we do not forget our traditional ways. If we did forget, the Washo will have to pay the price. We don't know what that price is, because we don't want to know; we don't want to pay that price. We have kept our traditions."

5 There are several caves at Cave Rock, high and low. The cannibals, the Tanu, were trapped by the Water Babies in the lowest one, now covered with water. Because the water level is not as high as it used to be, due to environmental factors, when the level started to drop during a recent drought, part of the lower cave became exposed to the air. Some believed this would anger the Water Babies and perhaps even release the angry spirits of the cannibals, and so measures were taken to raise the water level to where it remains today. It's considered a great gift for the Washo when they have much winter snow, because it will help the lake stay at its regular level, so that the Tanu, or at least their spirits, will not be disturbed. The upper cave is where the medicine people go to commune with the Me-tsung.

6 Even the selfish Coyote was concerned for the Water Babies, if only to save his own hide. Water Babies can journey in spirit and appear anywhere. So it's best to keep them happy, either with offerings of fruits, sacred songs, or other helpful means. As the Washo people pass a sacred water spot during a journey back and forth, they always leave an offering to appease and honor the Water Babies.

7 If Coyote and Weasel had followed the old trade routes, they would have come to the body of water now known as San Francisco Bay. Lake Tahoe is a twenty-one-mile lake along the boundary between California and Nevada. The snow-capped peaks surrounding it rise over three

One reason the Washo consider Cave Rock so sacred is that long ago a neighboring tribe of cannibals began to attack the peaceful Washo. They were called *Tanu*, or "strangers." The Washo were not accustomed to violence and prayed to Creator, which sent the powerful Water Babies to help them. The Water Babies showed themselves to the Tanu, the cannibals, and lured them into the lower of the two great caves, and they became trapped in the spirit lodge.[4] Then they made the waters of the lake rise many feet, until the cave was completely underwater.[5] There was a great celebration among the Washo, and to this day they treat Cave Rock and the Water Babies with the greatest respect.[6] It is said that to this day, the Washo have never gone to war with other tribes.

Coyote's little brother Weasel caught a Water Baby once, and it nearly destroyed the Washo people. Coyote had heard about a great body of water to the west, and wanted to explore it. Weasel kept whining, "I wanna go, I wanna go!" until finally Coyote, the great hunter and leader, gave in to his baby brother's demands and said, "Okay, you can come, but you have to behave!" They walked west over the high Sierras. They went down a trail through the San Joaquin Valley that led straight to a large bay near the ocean. It was the greatest body of water they had ever seen.[7]

(continued on page 175)

thousand feet above the surface of the lake. The ancient Native American trails from the lake to the bay area are still considered sacred paths, even though they are now paved highways.

Dashiw Wat-le (First Light), a Washo friend, commented, "We're the mountain Southern Washo, but the lake was our place to gather from spring to summer, to fish and hunt. When it was fall time, because Tahoe is very high, we traveled all over the Sierras, and into the Carson Valley where there is a warmer climate."

After a few days of hunting, they decided to turn around and go home. It was on the return home that Weasel saw what looked to him like a small woman, on a rock. His older brother said, "Don't you even think about it." He answered, "I'm not thinking about anything," as he rolled his eyes. His older brother warned him again, "You leave that alone."

Coyote went to hunt, so the younger brother went to see if he could talk to this Water Baby, and they ended up in a scuffle. He ended up grabbing the Water Baby, scalping her, taking her scalp, and because it was long blonde hair, which he had never seen, he put it in his pocket.

So they traveled back, and as they walked through the valley, the elder brother looked back and was shocked to see that the great body of water was following them.

"Did you do anything, little brother?"

"Oh no, I did nothing. I was just looking around."

So they traveled and started heading up the Sierras. He turned around and saw that the water was still coming. He was very adamant, saying, "What did you do?

Little Brother said, "Nothing. Don't you believe me?"

Whatever it was, Coyote didn't want the Washo people to pay the consequences. When he headed over the mountain, he entered into the valley of the Washo people. It was then that Little Weasel looked back at the water following them and knew it was because of what was in his pocket, and held onto it really tight. He was not going to let go of the hair he had taken as his prize possession.

(continued on page 177)

8 Lake Tahoe is fresh water, but, as the story implies, it is so big it looks almost like an ocean when you stand right up next to it. Like most stories in this book, it is punctuated near the end with a "Why?" story explanation, linking ever-present Creation, which is ongoing, and us.

Job's Peak is the highest peak in the Carson Valley area, and yet the water was approaching, climbing the side of the mountain. Then the older brother saw something dangling from the other one's pocket. He snatched it from Weasel. He said, "I told you, you cannot take this!" They got into a terrible fight. Even Coyote was not powerful enough to show disrespect to the Water Babies and get away with it. Now he understood why the water was following them all over the earth. The Water Babies were angry.

Weasel shuffled his feet and said, "Well, I did. It's mine and I want it. Now what do I do?"

Coyote said, "Well, you can't have it. There are some things in life you just cannot have. You must give it back for the safety and survival of the Washo people. We must return to the great water to the west!"

They went running back down the trail until they got to the water. Weasel went to the edge of the waterline and threw the hair back at the ocean. After the water came and took back the Water Baby's hair, the water started to recede. They say that all the waterways of the Sierras and the desert were what was left behind as the water started to recede and flow back to the ocean. That's how the Washo got all their ponds, lakes, waterfalls, and rivers. And, of course, Lake Tahoe is the biggest of those lakes left over from when Weasel angered the Water Babies and brought the ocean to the other side of the mountains.[8]

1 The *Ong* is a prehistoric bird of great size. Washo are proud of the ancientness of their village, and some believe that the Ong really was a descendant of the pterodactyl. Paleontologists would argue otherwise, but the Washo say they remember back to the *real* old days.

2 Some believe the Ong used Cave Rock as a winter dwelling place, which means it might have, at some point, run off either the Washo, who would otherwise have been living there, or the Water Babies.

3 The winning of the chief's daughter's hand in marriage appears in only one of two versions of this story. It is probably from a later time, showing outside influences, and yet it adds a "rite of passage" dimension to the story. Symbolically, the Ong expresses the shadow side of the cosmic bird, whose greatness we can achieve through spiritual knowledge. As the Washo man aspires to rise to greatness and gain access to power, he must first master his own shadow side, which will otherwise destroy him. Symbolically the Ong is there as a guardian of that power, to see if he is worthy of it.

4 There is a similar story among the neighboring Shoshone called "Weasel and Owl" about a monster owl that captures two brothers and takes them to his island. One of the men hides an arrowhead of flint in a corpse that the owl is eating and it kills the owl, and the brothers use one giant wing as a boat to escape the island. Cave Rock is made of a volcanic type of stone, so the "poisonous" arrowhead was most likely fashioned from Cave Rock.

Most birds do *not* close their eyes when they eat, so a good hunter would notice this as unusual. On the other hand, it might be a signal to the listener that the story is "all made up," and not of this world.

□ The Great Bird Ong (Washo)

A long time ago, a monstrous bird called the Ong[1] lived in a big nest in [a great tall pine tree in] the middle of Lake Tahoe.[2] This gigantic man-eating bird picked up unsuspecting Washo. These people, who had not heeded persistent warnings, ventured into open areas where the monster could easily see and capture them. The Washo greatly feared this monster bird, who was so powerful that the wind from his wings could bend the trees when he flew near shore.

One of the band chiefs had a beautiful daughter, and a certain young brave knew if he killed the monster bird he would be known for his bravery and strength, and could ask the chief for his daughter to marry.[3]

[One day, he walked out in the open and waited for the great bird to arrive, and] the Ong snatched this young Washo and took him high into the air. [The man had known that the bird had a habit of lifting its victims high in the air and dropping them before eating them, so he brought a coil of rope with him, and while the bird was taking him upwards into the sky, he lashed himself in the crook of the bird's giant claws, where the bird could not pull him out with his beak.] The bird took the man to the huge nest in the middle of the lake. The Washo man pretended to be dead, but watched the Ong carefully all the time. Luckily, the monster was not very hungry, and had another person to eat. As the Washo watched, he noticed that the Ong closed his eyes to chew. This habit gave the Washo an idea. Each time the Ong took a bite and closed his eyes, the Washo threw several [poisonous] arrowheads into its mouth.[4] By nightfall,

(continued on page 181)

5 In the "Weasel and Owl" story of the Shoshone, the brothers take one wing of the giant owl and, creating a makeshift boat, escape the island with their lives. Although this evokes the genre of fantasy, the Washo say there were some very large birds flying around many thousands of years ago, when their ancestors lived there.

6 Some would say that men have to go through dangerous male initiation rites, finding and owning their own power, looking at and mastering their own dark side, before they can be good husbands and fathers.

7 The story does not say where underneath the lake the skeleton lies, but one person I talked to believed you could probably see it from the very top of *De-ek Wadoppush,* which is difficult to reach unless you are a giant bird.

all these arrowheads had made the beast very sick. As the monster moaned and groaned with pain, a terrible storm raged. By morning, the Ong was dead. So the young Washo pulled a feather from Ong's tail and glided down from the nest, and using the feather as a boat,[5] he reached shore and returned home.[6] [From a certain high point on the mountain, they say you can still see the skeleton of the monster bird, lying at the bottom of the lake, and the stones and arrowheads he had eaten.][7]

10
The Spiritual Journey

☰ In this tale of life after death, the stone canoe, first of all, is a miraculous concept that defies the laws of nature. Upon hearing this story, children will ask, "But do stone boats float?" This paradox is a clue to the listener that the stone canoe is more than just a stone canoe: it is also a metaphor, a reference to something not physical and not of this world. It is "real" in a different sense.

When the Peacemaker first came to the territory of the Iroquois (Haudenosaunee), he sailed across Lake Ontario in a white stone canoe. He began carving it as a young boy and finished it upon coming of age. As the canoe represents the journey of life, this is an excellent metaphor for what today is called spiritual self-actualization.

Many Native American stories, not to mention Celtic stories, include a wedding-day death, as nothing could be more dramatic, sure to open the hearts of every listener. In this case, the warrior turns to the Path of Peace, like the other sailor of the white stone canoe, the Iroquois Peacemaker. In Algonquin culture (of which Ojibway is a prominent member nation) we call this the Way of the Heron, as the heron makes peace between other birds when they are fighting.

There is a door to the spirit world that opens whenever someone dies, and it is at these times that miraculous things happen. Many great souls, experiencing a great loss, have an epiphany and realize, like the Buddha, that there is never a reason to choose violence over peace. It is the way that the Great Spirit, who loves all its children equally, would prefer.

1 Visions are a natural part of life. It is said, "If you're not having visions, you're not living right." Some might add, "If you're not dreaming, you're not really awake." Some Native languages make little distinction between dreams when you are asleep and dreams when you are awake. Either way, "you saw it." With some elders, when they tell me stories of their day, I find myself constantly asking, "Was this while you were asleep or awake?"

2 In a great number of Native American traditions, the hair is cut in mourning. It is such a basic instinct that there is little explanation

☐ The Stone Canoe
(Ojibway/Anishinabi)

There was once a very beautiful young girl who died suddenly on the day she was to have been married to a handsome young man. He was also brave, but his heart was not strong enough to endure this loss. From the hour she was buried, there was no more joy or peace for him. He would often visit the spot where the women had buried her and sit there dreaming.[1]

Some of his friends thought he should try to forget his sorrow by hunting or by following the warpath. But war and hunting had lost their charms for him. His heart was already dead within him. He pushed aside both his war club and his bow and arrows, and he cut his hair in mourning.[2]

(continued on page 187)

needed. Cutting the hair is a way of self-purification, surrendering one's will to Creator's will. The hair is part of the body, the way feathers are part of the bird, and to use hair as an offering is considered very powerful. Both the Native American pipe carrier and the Nazirites in the Book of Exodus cut their hair in mourning and use it as an offering to God. It is said in Exodus that the Nazirites shall cut their hair when someone dies during their "time of separation," which is a thirty-day monastic period of prayer. This is most certainly a carry-over from the pre-Mosaic times of the tribal Hebrew nations. Moses would have known the story of Isis, Goddess of Egypt, who cut off a lock of her hair in mourning when her husband Osiris died, and similar Sumerian stories as well, such as the story about Astarte (Ishtar/Inanna) who cut her hair in mourning for Tammuz. In the cult of Tammuz, hair was cut in ceremonial mourning at each year's festival. It is clear that this was a prevalent "pagan" Hebrew custom as well, but it was outlawed by the priests. We can find admonishments for the people to stop in Jeremiah 16:6, Deuteronomy 14:1, Leviticus 19:27, and Leviticus 21:1–5. Nonverbal messages have always been sent to the world by how we wear our hair, dating back to the earliest times and in all places.

3 Each tribe has a different direction to which they say the path of souls leads. Some Ojibway say it goes to the west, and walk out a western door backward, saying "all my relations" (the phrase in Ojibway is difficult to translate precisely) so as not to tempt fate by walking face forward through the western door. The Mi'kmaq path of souls is to the east, "where the sun comes up"; the Lenape path is to the southwest, as is the Lakota. The Cherokee path of souls is to the west. I'm sure some travel to the north as well. What's important here is that the stories of the young man's traditions had been preparing him all along so that he would know what to do when his time came to travel that road. This teaches us that one's own traditions are very important to learn about. They can help us through many rites of passage.

He had heard the old people say there was a path that led to the land of souls, and he made up his mind to follow it. One morning, after having made his preparations for the journey, he picked up his bow and arrows, called to his dog, and started out. He hardly knew which way to go. He was only guided by the tradition that he must go south.[3]

As he walked along, he could see at first no change in the face of the country. Forests and hills and valleys and streams had the same look as they wore in his native place. There was snow on the ground, and sometimes it was even piled and matted on the thick trees and bushes. But after a long while it began to diminish, and finally disappeared. The forest took on a more cheerful appearance, the leaves put forth their buds, and before he was aware of the completeness of the change, he found himself surrounded by spring.

He had left behind him the land of snow and ice. The clouds of winter had rolled away from the sky. The air became mild. A pure field of blue was above him. As he went along he saw flowers beside his path and heard the songs of birds. By these signs he knew that he was going the right way, for they agreed with the traditions of his tribe.

(continued on page 189)

4 About 1000 B.C.E., many burial grounds were at grassy knolls, natural hills near groves of trees, away from where people tended to live. It is said that mound burials, which developed at that time, were in imitation of those knolls. The groves were often of oak, a tree associated with the ancestors, because before 1000 B.C.E., the old ones collected and ate ground nuts (acorns) during hard times. In Algonquin teachings, there is an old grandfather at the end of a long road who sits by a fire. He is at that place or portal that the souls of the living cannot go past. If they go through that door, they will never wake up back on earth. The old man in this story is apparently the brother of that one, and sits at another door, closer to earth, similar to the tunnel spoken of in Hindu cultures and in Raymond Moody's works on life after death, especially *Life after Life*.

5 This part of the story is very similar to stories from around the world about wizards. When we seek to find a prophet or a seer or guru, we should not be surprised when they say, "I know why you have come!" This was incorporated into the movie *The Wizard of Oz*, but only after ten thousand wonderful variations in every land on earth. When Joseph Epes Brown found Black Elk in a tent in a potato field, he felt rather anxious about approaching the elder without having been invited, as they had never met. They smoked a pipe together in silence. Brown writes in *The Sacred Pipe*, "When the ritual smoking was completed, the old man turned to me and asked why I had taken so long in getting there, for he had been expecting my coming. He then invited me to spend the winter with him and his extended family at their home on Wounded Knee Creek, Pine Ridge Reservation."

6 This passage is similar to Hindu and Sikh stories of *bhumis,* or inner planes, that often appear as endless rolling hills and fields. The dog represents the animal self (i.e., the human body). From the spirit world perspective, the human body is a thing, a possession we must take care of. It protects the soul in the cold earth world the way a dog protects a man. The bow represents the well-honed mind, which can project its thoughts over long distances, and the arrows represent those thoughts.

At length, he spied a path. It led him through a grove, then up a long, high ridge, on the very top of which stood a lodge. At the door was an old man with white hair, whose eyes, though deeply sunken, had a fiery brilliance. He had a long robe of skins thrown loosely around his shoulders and a staff in his hands.[4]

The young man began to tell his story. But the old chief stopped him before he had spoken ten words. "I have expected you," he said, "and had just risen to welcome you to my lodge. She whom you seek passed by here only a few days ago, and being tired from her journey, rested herself here. Enter my lodge and be seated. I will then answer your questions and give you directions for the remainder of your journey."[5]

When this was accomplished, the old chief brought the young man back out through the door of the lodge. "You see yonder lake?" he said. "And the wide-stretching blue plains beyond? It is the land of souls. You now stand on its borders, and my lodge is at the gate of entrance. But you cannot take your body along. Leave it here with your bow and arrows and your dog. You will find them safe on your return."[6]

So saying, he went back into the lodge, and the traveler bounded forward, as if his feet had suddenly been given the power of wings. But all things retained their natural colors and shapes. The woods and leaves, the streams and lakes, were only brighter and more beautiful than before. Animals bounded across his path with a freedom and confidence that seemed to tell him there was no bloodshed here. Birds of beautiful plumage lived in the groves and sported in the waters.

(continued on page 191)

When we enter the spirit world we must leave the mind "by the door" or we will not make the journey. We will be slowed down by too much thinking, and too encumbered by confusion. This story teaches us that it is not enough to drop just the body—we must quiet the mind as well when engaging the spirit world. This is a non-materialistic culture's way of saying "you can't take it with you!" Once we drop these burdens, our soul springs forth as if liberated from a great weight.

7 This is directly from Algonquin (specifically Ojibway) teachings about the nature of the soul. Surprisingly, most indigenous cultures around the world speak of a "shadow" soul and also a "blood" soul, which is the one closest to the body. It is the blood soul that can be stolen and used by bad spirits to haunt others, the way a ghost does. Cultures in Africa, Asia, and Native America, not to mention many others, "see" the soul in many parts. The shadow soul is a higher self, but we can also merge with the One Great Sun in which there is no shadow at all. That animals and trees have shadow souls too is in line with traditional Algonquin thought.

8 We are reminded of the ancient story of Orpheus, who searches the underworld for Euridice, retold over and over again with different characters. Throughout history, certain couples have become magically linked through the power of love, and this kind of love is the only thing that is stronger than death. The one left behind can still "find" his lover, or even at times "see through his lover's eyes," even though she is in the spirit world and he is in this material one. Likewise, we have all heard stories of the departed ones reaching out to us among the living, becoming a bird or a fragrance, or leaving a message in some way. It is as if that kind of love "awakens" a God-filled power within us.

This scene implies that they were "twin souls" and that they come from a similar "place" and will be able to travel and live together after death. The island is an ancient symbol in Algonquin culture, both a metaphor for the innermost circle, that which is guarded and protected, and also literally a place where the ancestors lived and gathered for important meetings.

There was one thing, however, that struck him as peculiar. He noticed that he was not stopped by trees or other objects. He seemed to walk directly through them. They were, in fact, merely the souls or shadows of real trees. He became aware that he was in a land of shadows.[7]

When he had traveled half a day's journey, through a country that grew more and more attractive, he came to the banks of a broad lake, in the center of which was a large and beautiful island. He found a canoe of shining white stone tied to the shore. He was now sure that he had followed the right path, for the aged man had told him of this. There were also shining paddles. He immediately got into the canoe, and had just taken the paddles into his hands when, to his joy and surprise, he beheld the object of his search in another canoe, exactly like his own in every respect. She had exactly imitated his motions, and they were side by side.[8]

At once they pushed out from the shore and began to cross the lake. Its waves seemed to be rising, and at a distance looked ready to swallow them up. But just as they came to the whitened edge of the first great wave, it seemed to melt away, as if it had been merely a shadow or a reflection. No sooner did they pass through one wreath of foam, however, than another still more threatening rose up. They were in constant fear. Moreover, through the clear water they could see the bones of many men who had perished strewn on the bottom of the lake.

(continued on page 193)

9 | In Native American tales, the experiences we have in the spirit world reflect those we created for ourselves in the earth world. In a Lenape story, the traveler on the path of souls must cross a turbulent river on a bridge of tricky rolling logs. It is a test of faith, and of concentration. To make it worse, there are wild dogs there; these dogs know and are in touch with the dogs you knew on earth. If you were good to those dogs on earth, they will help you. If you were bad to earth dogs and beat them, these dogs will tear you to pieces and eat you. I told this story to a Lakota man, and he made a terrible face. I said, "What's wrong?" He answered, "We eat dogs!" "Perhaps the buffalo will help you across!" I said. In *The Sacred Pipe*, it is retold that in Lakota belief, the departed walk along the spirit path we call the Milky Way until they meet an old woman named Maya Owichapaha, "she who pushes them over the bank." There the road divides; the good souls bear to the right and onward to *Wakan-Tanka;* the less satisfactory ones are pushed to the left (south) where they await further training.

Such rites of passage of the soul are common throughout the world. Apparently the slightest infractions of ethics on earth create "ripples" in the lakes there. There is a Celtic story about an angel who helps children across a scary bridge in the spirit world. Children are highly respected in Ojibway/Anishinabi and other Algonquin and Woodland Indian cultures. A door to the spirit world opens when babies are being born, and everyone feels it; six years or so later, they are still connected to the spirit world. Their zingy retorts and interruptions are often pondered very seriously, as their intuition is considered to be more accurate than that of adults. There is a widespread belief among Eastern Woodland people that many of those old souls who have worked out their problems in past lives come to earth, live pure, even miraculous lives, and die by mysterious causes just before reaching puberty. They thereby avoid getting entangled in further mistakes and obligations on earth, and it marks the last earthly life of such an enlightened soul. They then remain as watchers, to help the people, especially in times of sickness, grief, and soul-searching, such as this young man experienced. They are almost like angels, but have memories of being human and are

The Master of Life had decreed that the two of them should pass safely through, for they had both led good lives on earth. But they saw many others struggling and sinking in the waves. There were old men and young men, and women too. Some passed safely through, and some sank. But it was only the little children whose canoes seemed to meet no waves at all. Finally, every difficulty was passed, as if in an instant, and they both leaped out onto the happy island.[9]

(continued on page 195)

therefore very compassionate. They generally do not speak to those they are assisting.

[10] This is probably meant to be taken quite literally, as it follows closely with Algonquin/Anishinabi teachings about the spirit world where there is no hunger, where you can absorb the sustenance of life from the air.

[11] In some versions, he weeps upon awakening from his vision because "it was not real." But the point of the story is that the journey *was* real, and that it healed him in his heart; otherwise it would serve no purpose. Creator does not torment the innocent. Within the Algonquin/Anishinabi tradition, dreams and visions are no less real than waking life, just different, and they serve as medicine. For those who break through the barriers of *loowaywoodee* (*loo-***way**-*woo-***dee**), "bad things in my heart," such as confusion, fear, and anger, waking life and dream life become quite similar, interconnected and full of meaning.

Lama Norlha Rinpoche said that Native Americans are not so different from Tibetans, and that in old times, Native Americans "believed only half of what they could see and hear." I think this means they were mindful of the emptiness of physical reality, which is half dream, half illusion. They could see through the surface of reality's rippling lake and glimpse to the bottom. They could therefore do what I call Dream Walking, which is to merge inner and outer realities into one fluid reality. Shape shifting is only one small but dramatic aspect of this ability. Lama Norlha would call shape shifting (practiced by Milarepa, and other lamas of the Kagyu lineage) a stage of Mahamudra. Referring to a time when so many Native Americans have been thrown in and out of residential schools, gotten tangled up with the economics of the dominant culture, and lost touch with their visions, Lama Norlha continued, "Now most believe that all they see is real." This is the very goal that the residential schools have worked hard to achieve, to bring Native Americans into the "real world." But the masters, gurus, rinpoches, and sages of Asia agree, this is a tragic loss to the world.

They felt that the air was food. It strengthened and nourished them. They wandered over the blissful fields, where everything was made to please the eye and ear. There were no storms. There was no ice, no chilly wind. No one shivered for want of warm clothes. No one suffered from hunger, no one mourned the dead. They saw no graves. They heard of no wars. There was no hunting for animals, for the air itself was food.[10]

Gladly would the young warrior have remained there forever, but he was obliged to go back for his body. He did not see the Master of Life, but he heard his voice in a soft breeze. "Go back," said the voice, "to the land where you came from. Your time has not come yet. The duties for which I made you, and which you are to perform, are not yet finished. Return to your people and accomplish the duties of a good man. You will be sachem of your tribe for many winters. The rules you must observe will be told you by my messenger who keeps the gate. When he gives you back your body, he will tell you what to do. Listen to him, and you shall one day rejoin the spirit whom you must now leave behind. She has been accepted and will be here always, as young and as happy as she was when I first called her from the land of snows."

When the voice had ceased, the young man awoke. It had been a dream, and although he was still in the bitter land of snows, and hunger and tears, he knew he had been blessed by the Creator with a good vision. He felt his beloved standing next to him, smiling at him, saw her beauty with his heart, still shining like the moon, and knew that their time to be together had not come yet.[11]

▤ The resemblance between this story and the clinical studies by Dr. Raymond Moody of people who had experienced "life after death" is nothing short of remarkable. Moody interviewed those who had "died" on the operating table, and asked them what they had seen during that time, and noted that many of the stories from people around the world were similar, even if this experience directly contradicted their own religion. In many cases, the subjects were adamant that it had really happened, and could remember it all in brilliant detail. The majority of those who come back say they were told that their mission in life was not over, that they must live to fulfill that mission before they can return.

The word for "heaven" in most Algonkian tongues, and in other Native American languages and in Asia as well, is related to the word for "light." In Mi'kmaq the word is *wasowhy* (**wa**-*so*-**why**), "the whole big light." The Lenape have a story of a man who fell unconscious in the forest for sixteen days. When they revived him, he told them he was in a much happier world. Typically, he was not overjoyed to be back. He told them, "Next time I die, you people have a great big party for me, because I will be going to a very nice place, talking to my ancestors and having a great time!"

I myself have interviewed those who remember dying, going to a beautiful place, and coming back. Sometimes the disappointment of living on earth again is so great that the subjects develop feelings of rejection and failure. On the other hand, I had a music teacher who had lived a sad and unproductive life. He "died" from liver complications related to his lifelong alcoholism, but when he came back he was totally different. Filled with a visible light and unstoppable energy, he organized and trained a youth orchestra and chorus and toured the nation, singing songs about purpose in life. He's now back in that heavenly world, but I learned a lot from that man. I was the little guitarist in his orchestra!

Notes □

Preface

1. "What might we have made of the Indian?" Edward S. Curtis, *Thirty Years of Friendly Understanding*, quoted in Alma Hutchens, *Indian Herbology of North America* (1973; repr. Boston: Shambhala, 1991), xxiv.

2. Victor Mair, *The Tao Te Ching: The Classic Book of Integrity and the Way* (New York: Bantam Books, 1990), 132–34.

3. Othman Abd-ar-Rahman Llewellyn, "The Basis for a Discipline of Islamic Environmental Law," in *Islam and Ecology: A Bestowed Trust*, eds. Richard C. Foltz, Frederick Denny, and Azizan Baharuddin (Cambridge, MA: Harvard University Press, 2003), 190.

Introduction

1. Heinrich Zimmer, in *Myths and Symbols in Indian Art and Civilization,* ed. Joseph Campbell (New York: Harper Torch Books, 1946).

2. John Bierhorst, in *The White Deer: And Other Stories Told by the Lenape* (New York: William Morrow and Co., 1995), 10–11, writes: "Generally, the time for telling was after dark and almost always during the coldest months. That stories must be told only in winter is a very old rule, widespread in native America. Delawares used to say that if tales were told out of season, 'the bugs would chase you' or 'all the worms would take after you.' Some said the ground had to be frozen; if it were not, and if stories were told, snakes and lizards would crawl into bed with you. As explained by others, there should be stories only 'when things around cannot hear'—never in summer when 'everything is awake.'"

3. Michael H. Brown, "The Bone Game: A Native American Ritual for Developing Personal Power and Group or Tribal Consciousness," *Journal of Experiential Education* 13 (May 1990): 1. According to Robert Vetter, the Adinaha social version of the seed game is used to resolve family conflicts in Iroquoian (Haudenosaunee) society today.

4 Lynn Johnson, professor of anthropology at Vassar College, showed me what appeared to be a peach-pit platter that was found in a cave in the Aleutian Islands under a thick layer of debris, fox droppings, and dirt, indicating great antiquity.

5. Kathryn Gabriel, "Gambling and Spirituality, a New Anthropological Perspective," www.nmweddingphotos.com/articles/professional/myths.html #gamblinghasroots, article based on her book *Gambler Way: Indian Gaming in Mythology, History, and Archaeology in North America* (Boulder, CO: Johnson Books, 1996).

6. Quoted in Zimmer, 44.

7. Alexi Kondratiev, *Celtic Rituals: An Authentic Guide to Ancient Celtic Spirituality* (Scotland: New Celtic Publishing, 1999).

8. Eddie Benton Benaise, *The Mishomis Book (*St. Paul, MN: Indian Country Press, 1979), 17.

9. *The Sacred Pipe: Black Elk's Account of the Seven Rites of the Oglala Sioux, Recorded and Edited by Joseph Epes Brown* (Norman: University of Oklahoma Press, 1953), 16.

10. Robert Bly, *Iron John: A Book about Men* (Reading, MA: Addison-Wesley Publishers, 2002), 48.

11. Mary Pat Fisher, *Living Religions*, 5th ed. (Englewood Cliffs, NJ: Prentice Hall Publishers, 1990), 164. Just as important to the understanding of Buddhism is the following version from the Kagyu School of Tibetan Buddhism: "To the Buddha, the dharma, the sanga, the supreme assembly, I seek refuge until I attain enlightenment. Through the merit of my practice of generosity and the others may I accomplish Buddhahood for the benefit of beings."

12. Brown, "The Bone Game."

13. Joseph Campbell, *The Hero with a Thousand Faces* (1949; repr. Princeton: Princeton University Press, 1968), 292–93.

14. First Light, Washo tribal member, interviewed by author. Lake Tahoe is freshwater, but looks like the sea.

15. Zimmer, p. 101.

Creation Stories

THE MUD DIVER STORY

This version copyright © 2002 by Evan Pritchard, first performed in conjunction with a presentation on the banks of the Esopus River called "Esopus River Suite" by The Arm of the Sea Theater. There are many spellings of these Munsee words, and the spelling used here is consistent with the phonetic spellings developed by Stephen Augustine and Evan Pritchard in 1990 for Algonkian languages.

6. "with mud on its back": In a film documentary on stone structures in the Northeast by award-winning archaeologist Ted Timreck, I showed and spoke about a huge stone representation of a turtle, still standing in Lenape territory, whose facial features strongly suggest the Muhlenberg mud turtle, which

I believe to be a reference to Creation.

9. "continents on which humankind now lives": Henry Tall Bull, *Cheyenne Legends of Creation* (Billings, MT: Council for Indian Education, 1972). This Cheyenne version has been completely reworded here for literary purposes.

THE MAKING OF THE WORLD

Horatio Hale, "The Making of the World" (1888), reprinted in *American Indians: Folk Tales and Legends,* ed. Keith Cunningham. This is my own retelling.

9. "Hadiths teach respect": Foltz, 199.

The Wager for the World

THE CHICKADEE STORY

1. "Moongarm ... stains the heavens with blood": This story was originally published in 1884 in Charles G. Leland, *The Algonquin Legends of the Northeast, or Myths and Folklore of the Micmac, Passamaquoddy, and Penobscot Tribes* (London: S. Low, Marson, Searle, Rivington, 1884; repr. New York: Dover Publications, 1992).

THE ADOPTION OF THE HUMAN RACE

John Reed Swanton's version of this story was published in *Bureau of American Ethnology Bulletin* 42 (1924–25): 240 (GPO).

CO-NO, THE WORLD'S GREATEST GAMBLER

A different version of this story appears in Oliver La Mere, *Winnebago Stories* (New York: Rand McNally, 1928), 75.

The Origins of Fire

THE FIRST FIRE

This Cherokee story is based on the version written down by James Mooney of the Bureau of American Ethnology of the Smithsonian Institution and his assistant Cherokee elder Will West Long, while interviewing Cherokee (Tsalagi) elders on the Qualla Reservation at Big Cove, North Carolina. Assumed to be quite ancient, it was published in 1900 under the title *The Myths of the Cherokee* in the nineteenth annual *Report of the Bureau of American Ethnology*.

1. "The Cherokee say": *The Native American Traditional Code of Ethics,* April 2000, is available on the website of the Southern Band of Cherokees www.southernband.org.

3. "islands in rivers": My forthcoming book *Islands of Fire* will explore the tradi-

tion of Native Americans holding council fire meetings on islands in rivers, including Hennepin Island, near St. Paul, Minnesota, in the Mississippi River; Minisink Island(s) in the Delaware River; Wheeling Island in the Ohio River; Schodack Island in the Hudson River near Albany, New York; Saco Island in the Saco River; Belle Island in the James River at Richmond, Virginia; and Roosevelt Island in the Potomac River near Washington, D.C. The list of examples is endless. All of these were used for council fires at first contact, and most have become state capitals. In other words, they are still places of power today. In the territory of the old Cherokee, here are some candidates for islands in rivers at prominent trail crossings: Browntown Island (site of the Chattanooga airport) in the Tennessee River in Knoxville; Williams Island in the Tennessee River in Chattanooga; and Burns Island, farther west from Chattanooga, on the Alabama border. It was here, probably on Burns Island, that de Soto encountered some Creek Indians called the Chiaha. He wrote that they were subject to the chief of Coca. They spoke Hitchiti.

"He Who is in Heaven will show compassion to you.": Llewellyn, "The Basis for a Discipline of Islamic Environmental Law," 189.

FIRE-STEALING FOX

A version of this story was published by Frank Russell in *Journal of American Folk Lore* 11 (1898): 261–62.

The Sacred Pipe

WHITE BUFFALO CALF WOMAN

This story was first published by George A. Dorsey in "Legend of the Teton Sioux Medicine Pipe," *Journal of American Folk Lore* 19/20 (1906): 326.

7. "We will undo nothing that we have done": This story is told by George Bird Grinnell in *Pawnee, Blackfoot and Cheyenne: History and Folklore of the Plains* (New York: Scribners, 1961), 121.

"the most sacred object in North America": More information regarding this controversy can be found on the website www.manataka.org./page228.html.

"Why?" Stories

HOW DEER GOT HIS HORNS

Like "The First Fire," "How Deer Got His Horns" was written down by James Mooney of the Bureau of American Ethnology of the Smithsonian Institution and his assistant Cherokee Will West Long and published in 1900.

WHY THE BLACKFEET NEVER KILL MICE

A version of the story called "Why the Blackfeet Don't Kill Mice" was published
by Frank B. Linderman (Coskeeseecocot), in *Indian Why Stories: Sparks From
War Eagle's Lodge Fire,* illus. Charles M. Russell (Cahnetawahseenaeket) (New
York: Charles Scribner's Sons, 1915), 65.

The Sacred Hero

SON OF LIGHT DEFEATS THE MONSTER

A version called "Son of Light Kills the Monster" (Hopi) by Alexander Stephen was
published in the *Journal of American Folk Lore* 42 (1929), 2 (GPO).

18. "walked away in defeat": This story appears in Charles G. Leland, *Algonquin
Legends,* 58–59.

The Return of the Sun

LITTLE BROTHER GETS MAD AT THE SUN

4. "Homo floresiensis used tools": "Asian Odyssey," *National Geographic,* April
2005, 16.

Coyotes and Other Tricksters

"Deer and Blue Jay," "Coyote and Wren," and "Coyote and the Salmon," were
stories told by Chief Eaglewing, a Klamath Indian of northern California who
attended Indian schools at Hoopa and Riverside. Although charming and fun,
his stories are also full of ancient and authentic teachings. His versions were
published in *Peek-wa Stories by Chief Eaglewing* (Grover C. Sanderson) in
1938.

Nature Spirits, Landkeepers, and Tribal Guardians

THE MEESANG, OR WATER BABIES

The core material of this story was published under the title "Water Babies" by
Stephen Powers in an 1877 U.S. government publication called *Tribes of California* (AMS Reprints Press, 1976), 338. The story has been corrected and
augmented for this edition with the assistance of First Light, a Washo elder.

THE GREAT BIRD ONG

This story appears in Edward S. Curtis, *The North American Indian* (1907–30; repr.
New York: Johnson Reprint Co.), 25:150–51. First Light also provided extensive corrections and details for the version here.

The Spiritual Journey

THE STONE CANOE

An early version of this story was collected by Henry Rowe Schoolcraft and appears in *The Fire Plume: Legends of the American Indians,* ed. John Bierhorst (New York: Dial Press, 1969).

"other birds when they are fighting": This information was told to me by William Commanda and several other elders in 1998.

5. "spend the winter": Brown, p. xii.

"talking to my ancestors and having a great time!": This is recounted by John Bierhorst in *Mythology of the Lenape: Guide and Texts* (Tucson: Arizona University Press, 1995), 28-29, and is included in my book *Native New Yorkers* (San Francisco: Council Oak Books, 2001).

Note to the reader: After diligently searching and using every effort to secure permissions from field sources and copyright proprietors, the author regrets any errors or omissions, and asks that any errors or omissions be brought to his attention so they may be corrected in future editions.

Acknowledgments ☐

There are many people who have helped me during the completion of this manuscript. First I would like to thank my parents for their patient encouragement and research assistance. I would also like to thank the people of SkyLight Paths and Andrew Harvey for their vision of creating a cross-cultural spiritual dialogue through the written word, and Maura Shaw, my editor, for her hard work on this book. It was her tireless pursuit of a Native American collection of annotated stories to add to this acclaimed series that inspired me to agree to begin the process. Her vision concerning the importance of this volume inspired me to dig deeper for mythopoetic meaning. Thanks also to project editor Mark Ogilbee for his patience, especially in the final stages of this book. There are so many others to thank for making this experience more enjoyable, I will list them alphabetically.

Eddie Benton Benaise, for the Four Gifts teachings of the Ojibway, the Fire Keeper story, and much, much more. His *Mishomis Book* is a classic text of the Anishinabi People.

William Commanda for his profound inspiration to all Native American storytellers.

First Light *(Dashiw Wat-le)* for sharing her knowledge of the Washo tales with the world.

Ken Gale for assistance with my Jack Kirby research.

Tiokasin Ghosthorse for providing many insights concerning the sacred pipe and differences between Lakota and Dakota traditions.

Miguel Gonzales for Bushido teachings.

Historian Karen Hitt for book loans, especially the Klamath stories.

Terri Leonino and Greg Artzner for alerting me to *Shomrei Adama.*

Alexi Kondratief for insights into Son of Light via his book *Celtic Rituals.*

Vernon Newton for sharing with me his vast book collection.

Kay Olan for background and fact-checking on Haudenosaunee culture.

Joanne Plamondon for her chapter page designs and much enthusiasm.

Julia Porter for information on Ukrainian shamanism.

Lynn Pritchard for the chipmunk story and for introducing me to her raptor friends.

Monique Renaud for thunderbird teachings.

Raymundo Rodriguez for doughnuts, cowries, and turtles.

Laurie Scott for Algonkian assistance and book loans from her library.

Barbara James Snyder for her help with Washo stories.

Ted Timreck for expanding my horizons backward into time.

Peggy Turco (Ani Yeshe Palmo) of KTC for assistance with Tibetan–Native American comparisons.

Dr. Robert Vetter of Journeys into Indian Country for his assistance concerning Native American games.

Kristen Vincent for information on Vedic ritual.

Patrick Wadden and Marlena Maraleo for commissioning me to write the version of "The Mud Diver Story" included here.

Mike Watkins for showing me the Delaware traditions are alive and well.

White Eagle for Blackfoot-like mice teachings.

Brian Wilkes and www.standingbearfoundation.org for Cherokee teachings and for assistance with www.algonquinculture.org.

Inspiration

The Rebirthing of God
Christianity's Struggle for New Beginnings
By John Philip Newell

Drawing on modern prophets from East and West, and using the holy island of Iona as an icon of new beginnings, Celtic poet, peacemaker and scholar John Philip Newell dares us to imagine a new birth from deep within Christianity, a fresh stirring of the Spirit.
6 x 9, 160 pp, HC, 978-1-59473-542-4 **$19.99**

Finding God Beyond Religion: A Guide for Skeptics, Agnostics & Unorthodox Believers Inside & Outside the Church
By Tom Stella; Foreword by The Rev. Canon Marianne Wells Borg

Reinterprets traditional religious teachings central to the Christian faith for people who have outgrown the beliefs and devotional practices that once made sense to them.
6 x 9, 160 pp, Quality PB, 978-1-59473-485-4 **$16.99**

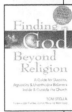

Fully Awake and Truly Alive: Spiritual Practices to Nurture Your Soul
By Rev. Jane E. Vennard; Foreword by Rami Shapiro

Illustrates the joys and frustrations of spiritual practice, offers insights from various religious traditions and provides exercises and meditations to help us become more fully alive.
6 x 9, 208 pp, Quality PB, 978-1-59473-473-1 **$16.99**

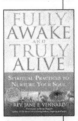

Journeys of Simplicity: Traveling Light with Thomas Merton, Bashō, Edward Abbey, Annie Dillard & Others *By Philip Harnden*

Invites you to consider a more graceful way of traveling through life. PB includes journal pages to help you get started on your own spiritual journey.
5 x 7¼, 144 pp, Quality PB, 978-1-59473-181-5 **$12.99**
5 x 7¼, 128 pp, HC, 978-1-893361-76-8 **$16.95**

Perennial Wisdom for the Spiritually Independent
Sacred Teachings—Annotated & Explained
Annotation by Rami Shapiro; Foreword by Richard Rohr

Weaves sacred texts and teachings from the world's major religions into a coherent exploration of the five core questions at the heart of every religion's search.
5½ x 8½, 336 pp, Quality PB, 978-1-59473-515-8 **$16.99**

Saving Civility: 52 Ways to Tame Rude, Crude & Attitude for a Polite Planet
By Sara Hacala

Provides fifty-two practical ways you can reverse the course of incivility and make the world a more enriching, pleasant place to live.
6 x 9, 240 pp, Quality PB, 978-1-59473-314-7 **$16.99**

Spiritually Healthy Divorce: Navigating Disruption with Insight & Hope
By Carolyne Call

A spiritual map to help you move through the twists and turns of divorce.
6 x 9, 224 pp, Quality PB, 978-1-59473-288-1 **$16.99**

Spirituality

The Forgiveness Handbook
Spiritual Wisdom and Practice for the Journey to Freedom, Healing and Peace
By the Editors at SkyLight Paths; Introduction by The Rev. Canon Marianne Wells Borg
Offers inspiration, encouragement and spiritual practice from across faith traditions for all who seek hope, wholeness and the freedom that comes from true forgiveness.
6 x 9, 256 pp, Quality PB, 978-1-59473-577-6 **$18.99**

Like a Child
Restoring the Awe, Wonder, Joy and Resiliency of the Human Spirit
By Rev. Timothy J. Mooney
By breaking free from our misperceptions about what it means to be an adult, we can reshape our world and become harbingers of grace. This unique spiritual resource explores Jesus's counsel to become like children in order to enter the kingdom of God. 6 x 9, 160 pp, Quality PB, 978-1-59473-543-1 **$16.99**

The Passionate Jesus: What We Can Learn from Jesus about Love, Fear, Grief, Joy and Living Authentically
By The Rev. Peter Wallace
Reveals Jesus as a passionate figure who was involved, present, connected, honest and direct with others and encourages you to build personal authenticity in every area of your own life. 6 x 9, 208 pp, Quality PB, 978-1-59473-393-2 **$18.99**

Gathering at God's Table: The Meaning of Mission in the Feast of Faith
By Katharine Jefferts Schori
A profound reminder of our role in the larger frame of God's dream for a restored and reconciled world. 6 x 9, 256 pp, HC, 978-1-59473-316-1 **$21.99**

The Heartbeat of God: Finding the Sacred in the Middle of Everything
By Katharine Jefferts Schori; Foreword by Joan Chittister, OSB
Explores our connections to other people, to other nations and with the environment through the lens of faith.
6 x 9, 240 pp, HC, 978-1-59473-292-8 **$21.99**

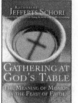

A Dangerous Dozen: Twelve Christians Who Threatened the Status Quo but Taught Us to Live Like Jesus
By the Rev. Canon C. K. Robertson, PhD; Foreword by Archbishop Desmond Tutu
Profiles twelve visionary men and women who challenged society and showed the world a different way of living.
6 x 9, 208 pp, Quality PB, 978-1-59473-298-0 **$16.99**

Laugh Your Way to Grace: Reclaiming the Spiritual Power of Humor
By Rev. Susan Sparks
A powerful, humorous case for laughter as a spiritual, healing path.
6 x 9, 176 pp, Quality PB, 978-1-59473-280-5 **$16.99**

Claiming Earth as Common Ground: The Ecological Crisis through the Lens of Faith
By Andrea Cohen-Kiener; Foreword by Rev. Sally Bingham
6 x 9, 192 pp, Quality PB, 978-1-59473-261-4 **$16.99**

Living into Hope: A Call to Spiritual Action for Such a Time as This
By Rev. Dr. Joan Brown Campbell; Foreword by Karen Armstrong
6 x 9, 208 pp, Quality PB, 978-1-59473-436-6 **$18.99**; HC, 978-1-59473-283-6 **$21.99**

Renewal in the Wilderness
A Spiritual Guide to Connecting with God in the Natural World
By John Lionberger 6 x 9, 176 pp, b/w photos, Quality PB, 978-1-59473-219-5 **$16.99**

Spiritual Adventures in the Snow
Skiing & Snowboarding as Renewal for Your Soul
By Dr. Marcia McFee and Rev. Karen Foster; Foreword by Paul Arthur
5½ x 8½, 208 pp, Quality PB, 978-1-59473-270-6 **$16.99**

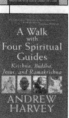

A Walk with Four Spiritual Guides: Krishna, Buddha, Jesus, and Ramakrishna
By Andrew Harvey 5½ x 8½, 192 pp, b/w photos & illus., Quality PB, 978-1-59473-138-9 **$15.99**

Spiritual Practice—The Sacred Art of Living Series

Dreaming—The Sacred Art: Incubating, Navigating & Interpreting
Sacred Dreams for Spiritual & Personal Growth
By Lori Joan Swick
This fascinating introduction to sacred dreams celebrates the dream experience as a way to deepen spiritual awareness and as a source of self-healing. Designed for the novice and the experienced sacred dreamer of all faith traditions, or none.
5½ x 8½, 224 pp, Quality PB, 978-1-59473-544-8 **$16.99**

Conversation—The Sacred Art: Practicing Presence in an Age of Distraction
By Diane M. Millis, PhD; Foreword by Rev. Tilden Edwards, PhD
5½ x 8½, 192 pp, Quality PB, 978-1-59473-474-8 **$16.99**

Dance—The Sacred Art: The Joy of Movement as a Spiritual Practice
By Cynthia Winton-Henry 5½ x 8½, 224 pp, Quality PB, 978-1-59473-268-3 **$16.99**

Fly-Fishing—The Sacred Art: Casting a Fly as a Spiritual Practice
By Rabbi Eric Eisenkramer and Rev. Michael Attas, MD; Foreword by Chris Wood, CEO, Trout Unlimited; Preface by Lori Simon, executive director, Casting for Recovery
5½ x 8½, 160 pp, Quality PB, 978-1-59473-299-7 **$16.99**

Giving—The Sacred Art: Creating a Lifestyle of Generosity
By Lauren Tyler Wright 5½ x 8½, 208 pp, Quality PB, 978-1-59473-224-9 **$16.99**

Haiku—The Sacred Art: A Spiritual Practice in Three Lines
By Margaret D. McGee 5½ x 8½, 192 pp, Quality PB, 978-1-59473-269-0 **$16.99**

Hospitality—The Sacred Art: Discovering the Hidden Spiritual Power of Invitation
and Welcome *By Rev. Nanette Sawyer; Foreword by Rev. Dirk Ficca*
5½ x 8½, 208 pp, Quality PB, 978-1-59473-228-7 **$16.99**

Labyrinths from the Outside In, 2nd Edition
Walking to Spiritual Insight—A Beginner's Guide *By Rev. Dr. Donna Schaper and Rev. Dr. Carole Ann Camp* 6 x 9, 208 pp, b/w illus. and photos, Quality PB, 978-1-59473-486-1 **$16.99**

Lectio Divina—**The Sacred Art**
Transforming Words & Images into Heart-Centered Prayer
By Christine Valters Paintner, PhD 5½ x 8½, 240 pp, Quality PB, 978-1-59473-300-0 **$16.99**

Pilgrimage—The Sacred Art: Journey to the Center of the Heart
By Dr. Sheryl A. Kujawa-Holbrook 5½ x 8½, 240 pp, Quality PB, 978-1-59473-472-4 **$16.99**

Practicing the Sacred Art of Listening
A Guide to Enrich Your Relationships and Kindle Your Spiritual Life
By Kay Lindahl 8 x 8, 176 pp, Quality PB, 978-1-893361-85-0 **$18.99**

Recovery—The Sacred Art: The Twelve Steps as Spiritual Practice *By Rami Shapiro*
Foreword by Joan Borysenko, PhD* 5½ x 8½, 240 pp, Quality PB, 978-1-59473-259-1 **$16.99**

Running—The Sacred Art: Preparing to Practice *By Dr. Warren A. Kay*
Foreword by Kristin Armstrong* 5½ x 8½, 160 pp, Quality PB, 978-1-59473-227-0 **$16.99**

The Sacred Art of Chant: Preparing to Practice
By Ana Hernández 5½ x 8½, 192 pp, Quality PB, 978-1-59473-036-8 **$16.99**

The Sacred Art of Fasting: Preparing to Practice
By Thomas Ryan, CSP 5½ x 8½, 192 pp, Quality PB, 978-1-59473-078-8 **$15.99**

The Sacred Art of Forgiveness: Forgiving Ourselves and Others through God's Grace
By Marcia Ford 8 x 8, 176 pp, Quality PB, 978-1-59473-175-4 **$18.99**

The Sacred Art of Listening: Forty Reflections for Cultivating a Spiritual Practice
By Kay Lindahl; Illus. by Amy Schnapper 8 x 8, 160 pp, b/w illus., Quality PB, 978-1-893361-44-7 **$16.99**

The Sacred Art of Lovingkindness: Preparing to Practice
By Rabbi Rami Shapiro; Foreword by Marcia Ford 5½ x 8½, 176 pp, Quality PB, 978-1-59473-151-8 **$16.99**

Thanking & Blessing—The Sacred Art: Spiritual Vitality through Gratefulness
By Jay Marshall, PhD; Foreword by Philip Gulley 5½ x 8½, 176 pp, Quality PB, 978-1-59473-231-7 **$16.99**

Writing—The Sacred Art: Beyond the Page to Spiritual Practice
By Rami Shapiro and Aaron Shapiro 5½ x 8½, 192 pp, Quality PB, 978-1-59473-372-7 **$16.99**

About SKYLIGHT PATHS Publishing

SkyLight Paths Publishing is creating a place where people of different spiritual traditions come together for challenge and inspiration, a place where we can help each other understand the mystery that lies at the heart of our existence.

Through spirituality, our religious beliefs are increasingly becoming a part of our lives—rather than *apart* from our lives. While many of us may be more interested than ever in spiritual growth, we may be less firmly planted in traditional religion. Yet, we do want to deepen our relationship to the sacred, to learn from our own as well as from other faith traditions, and to practice in new ways.

SkyLight Paths sees both believers and seekers as a community that increasingly transcends traditional boundaries of religion and denomination—people wanting to learn from each other, *walking together, finding the way.*

For your information and convenience, at the back of this book we have provided a list of other SkyLight Paths books you might find interesting and useful. They cover the following subjects:

Buddhism / Zen
Catholicism
Chaplaincy
Children's Books
Christianity
Comparative
  Religion
Earth-Based
  Spirituality
Enneagram
Global Spiritual
  Perspectives

Gnosticism
Hinduism /
  Vedanta
Inspiration
Islam / Sufism
Judaism
Meditation
Mindfulness
Monasticism
Mysticism
Personal Growth

Poetry
Prayer
Religious Etiquette
Retirement & Later-
  Life Spirituality
Spiritual Biography
Spiritual Direction
Spirituality
Women's Interest
Worship

Printed in the USA
CPSIA information can be obtained
at www.ICGtesting.com
JSHW022216140824
68134JS00018B/1094